Bruno Alves

Holocaustizing Bosnia

How the Holocaust Analogy Conditioned the Journalistic Discourse on the 1992-1995 Bosnian War

VDM Verlag Dr. Müller

Imprint

Bibliographic information by the German National Library: The German National Library lists this publication at the German National Bibliography; detailed bibliographic information is available on the Internet at
http://dnb.d-nb.de.

Cover image: www.purestockx.com

Published 2008 Saarbrücken

Publisher:
VDM Verlag Dr. Müller Aktiengesellschaft & Co. KG , Dudweiler Landstr. 125 a,
66123 Saarbrücken, Germany,
Phone +49 681 9100-698, Fax +49 681 9100-988,
Email: info@vdm-verlag.de

Produced in Germany by:
Reha GmbH, Dudweilerstrasse 72, D-66111 Saarbrücken
Schaltungsdienst Lange o.H.G., Zehrensdorfer Str. 11, 12277 Berlin, Germany
Books on Demand GmbH, Gutenbergring 53, 22848 Norderstedt, Germany

Impressum

Bibliografische Information der Deutschen Nationalbibliothek: Die Deutsche Nationalbibliothek verzeichnet diese Publikation in der Deutschen Nationalbibliografie; detaillierte bibliografische Daten sind im Internet über http://dnb.d-nb.de abrufbar.

Coverbild: www.purestockx.com

Erscheinungsjahr: 2008
Erscheinungsort: Saarbrücken

Verlag: VDM Verlag Dr. Müller Aktiengesellschaft & Co. KG , Dudweiler Landstr. 125 a,
D- 66123 Saarbrücken,
Telefon +49 681 9100-698, Telefax +49 681 9100-988,
Email: info@vdm-verlag.de

Herstellung in Deutschland:
Schaltungsdienst Lange o.H.G., Zehrensdorfer Str. 11, D-12277 Berlin
Books on Demand GmbH, Gutenbergring 53, D-22848 Norderstedt
Reha GmbH, Dudweilerstrasse 72, D-66111 Saarbrücken

ISBN: 978-3-639-05978-6

Abstract

The journalistic coverage of the 1992-1995 war in Bosnia-Herzegovina employed a strict discursive strategy that equated the events and the main protagonists of a complex civil war with a re-enactment of the Nazi Holocaust. Aiming to discover just how widespread was the use of the Holocaust analogy in the journalistic coverage of the conflict and what was its nature, this dissertation analysed *The Guardian* and the *Daily Mail* in two important weeks of this conflict: August 7th-14th 1992 – the week the Serb 'concentration' camps were exposed - and July 13th-20th 1995 – the week of the infamous Srebrenica massacre. After defining the expressions that fit into our 'Holocaust category', we used quantitative methods to ascertain just how present it was in these two weeks of coverage. We also employed qualitative methods – revolving around critical linguistics and critical discourse analysis – to analyse how this analogy affected the articles in which it was employed and how this fit into our theoretical discussion. In the end, we concluded that the Holocaust analogy was the dominant discursive strategy, regardless of whether it was used directly by the journalist or attributed to a third party. But when it was adopted directly by the journalists writing the stories, it thoroughly depoliticized the reported events and reduced them to a timeless struggle between 'Good' and 'Evil', confirming some of the theories discussed in this dissertation. We thus argue that while its overwhelming presence made the Holocaust analogy the dominant discursive strategy, its direct adoption by the journalists writing the stories made it the *unequivocal* way to interpret the Bosnian conflict.

Table of Contents

Introduction

English persons, therefore, of humanitarian and reformist disposition constantly went out to the Balkan Peninsula to see who was in fact ill-treating whom, and, being by the very nature of their perfectionist faith unable to accept the horrid hypothesis that everybody was ill-treating everybody else, all came back with a pet Balkan people established in their hearts as suffering and innocent, eternally the massacree and never the massacrer. Rebecca West, 1938

26th of February 2007. Ask any *connoisseur* of international law about the significance of this date and the answer is likely to come trickling down the tip of their tongue: it is the date when the International Court of Justice (ICJ), the UN's highest court, produced a sentence on the historic lawsuit filed by Bosnia against its neighbour, Serbia, seeking to cast it as a genocidal state and demanding hefty war reparations for damages caused in the 1992-1995 Bosnian war. The case is historical because it was the first time that a state sought the World Court to decide on whether a country could be considered guilty of genocide. That the country in question was Serbia, long seen by the international community as the main aggressor in *all* the Yugoslav conflicts and with a war record so barbarous that it was often compared to Nazi Germany in its brutality, gave the sentence an extra layer of historical *gravitas*. For a country that had already been found guilty in the court of world public opinion, the ICJ's sentence offered Serbia either the final nail in the coffin, or an unprecedented chance at salvation. What the World Court offered on the 26th of February 2007, in its complex and lengthy ruling, turned out to be a bit of both: while the court cleared Serbia of any direct responsibility for genocide and complicity in genocide during the three year Bosnian war it found Serbia guilty of failing to prevent the infamous Srebrenica massacre, led by Bosnian Serb paramilitary units, an act of genocide which resulted in the deaths of 8000 Muslim boys and men. Thus while Serbia was absolved of being a *de jure* genocidal nation it was still tainted with genocide by failing to use its influence to stop the Srebrenica killings, a grave violation of international law.

If Bosnia was predictably disappointed by this outcome, it is perhaps less predictable that another powerful actor in the Bosnian conflict would react in much the same way: the international news media. In fact, the international media were the first to massively expose Serb barbarity when, in the summer of 1992, the emaciated picture of Fikret Alic hit the world's television screens among hundreds of other men standing behind barbed wire at the detention camp of Trnopolje. But the importance of the media in reporting this war derives not only from being at the forefront of denouncing Serb horrors but also, and perhaps more importantly, from the way they were denounced. From Roy Guttman's *Newsday* story about 'The Death Camps of Bosnia', to ITN's evocative pictures of skeletal Muslims imprisoned in a barbed wire camp, culminating with the British tabloids' screaming headlines of 'Belsen 92', the war in Bosnia suddenly became a re-enactment of the world's most horrifying conflict: World War II. In this sense, the Serb aggressor became increasingly identified with the Nazis: he ran concentration camps (some even called them death camps); he was rumoured to be responsible for thousands of summary executions and countless rapes; he had a dream of a 'Greater Serbia' and was executing it with a ruthless strategy of 'ethnic cleansing'; he put people on trains and deported them to other countries after forcing them to sign over all their property; in short, all the evidence seemed to point that Serbia was sponsoring a 'Final Solution' type of strategy in Bosnia, preparing, in effect, to rid the country of all its Muslims.

This meant that, in a way, the Bosnian Muslims became the undisputed victims of the conflict, and, in many ways, the 'new Jews' of Europe, persecuted ruthlessly while the rest of the world once again stood by and watched, doing nothing. The final proof of Serbian intention was presented to the world in another summer, this time in July of 1995, when Serb paramilitary forces, led by General Radko Mladic, also known as the 'Butcher of Bosnia', overran the United Nations (UN) safe area of Srebrenica and proceeded, over the course of a few days, to systematically exterminate 8000 members of its male population, while Dutch UN soldiers, vastly outnumbered, stood by and watched. Largely described as 'Europe's worst massacre since World War II', Srebrenica had already been classified as a genocidal act by the International Tribunal for the former Yugoslavia (ICTY), before having its status confirmed by the ICJ.

So while Serbia has been acquitted of genocide by the World Court, it is arguably not unfair to state that it remains very much guilty, or at least highly suspicious, in the eyes of a large segment of the world media, and possibly, also of the world population. Why is this so? Much of this could have to do with the way in which journalists reported on the war in the first place, and especially with the established journalistic framework which equated the Serb's actions over the Bosnian Muslims with a modern day re-enactment of the Holocaust. Which brings us to the main topic of this dissertation: What are the implications of using the Holocaust analogy in the journalistic coverage of the Bosnian war? In order to ascertain this, we decided to address two main research questions: Firstly, "To what extent was the journalistic coverage of the Bosnian war 'Holocaustized'?"; and secondly, "What was the nature of this 'Holocaustization'?", in two of Britain's most famous daily newspapers: *The Guardian* and the *Daily Mail*.

In this sense, it should be noted that this dissertation falls squarely inside the media studies domain, particularly in the field of news discourse analysis, to which it hopes to contribute by investigating how the use of this exceptionally potent historical comparison conditioned the journalistic discourse on this Balkan conflict. What this dissertation does not intend, is to in any way minimize Serb guilt in the Bosnian conflict, or to whitewash any atrocities committed by the Bosnian Serbs and those who supported them. Nor does it intend to cast any doubt on the demonstrated fact that the Bosnian Serbs and their sponsors were chiefly responsible for the majority of the atrocities committed during this conflict. It seeks merely to discuss a part of the journalistic coverage of this war – two weeks in the summers of 1992 and 1995 respectively - and to find out what were the consequences of the approach chosen by the majority of its journalists.

To say that the journalistic coverage of the 1992-1995 Bosnian war was a fertile period in the annals of the journalistic profession is an understatement. Though it was not the first time journalists became actors in a war they were covering – a practice which arguably dates back to the birth of war journalism (Knightley, 2003) – there were many interesting developments, not the least of which was one journalist's theorization of the need for moral attachment in certain situations (Bell, 1998). But to fully understand what consequences such discursive practices may have one has to first hint at the complexity of the subject matter. A brief description of the Bosnian conflict will suffice at revealing the maze-like intricacies of this war.

The third, and arguably the deadliest, of the initial conflicts that erupted as the result of the disintegration of the former Yugoslavia – the first two were the ten day Slovenian war of secession and the Croatian war, still unresolved when the fighting broke out in Bosnia – the Bosnian war was, from the start, the conflict that had the greater potential for explosive violence. An independent nation only in medieval times, Bosnia-Herzegovina's "death sentence [...] was passed in the middle of December 1991 when Germany announced that it would recognize Slovenia and Croatia unconditionally on 15 January 1992" (Glenny, 1996: 163). This left the country, made up of a plurality of ethnic groups where the Muslim majority only outnumbered the Serbs by half-a-million people (Boyd, 1995: 25), with three basic choices, all of them conducive to warfare: Firstly, to stay inside rump Yugoslavia under the control of Milosevic and Serbia; secondly, to accept a territorial division between its two larger neighbours – Croatia and Serbia – as suggested by their respective presidents; and lastly, to become an independent state (Glenny, 1996: 143). "The Croats and the Muslims considered the first solution unacceptable; the Moslems and Yugoslavs, the second; and the Serbs, the third" (Glenny, 1996: 144). But when the then European Community (EC), pushed by Germany, decided to internationally recognize Croatia and Slovenia, Bosnia's Muslim president, Alija Izetbegovic, was emboldened to seek independence for his country. However, he made one crucial mistake: he did not secure "prior agreement from the Serbs" (Glenny, 1996: 164) – a significant part of Bosnia's landscape. This was exceptionally problematic, especially when one considers that, during the "Second World War [...] the genocidal struggle between Serbs and Croats was felt most keenly in Bosnia" with the aggravating fact that "the majority of Moslems co-operated with the Croat Fascists" (Glenny, 1996: 140) in exterminating the Serbs. The only reason the three communities were kept side by side in Tito's Yugoslavia is because they were forced to coexist, often times by violence, and because a system of tri-national parity was instituted that, at its apogee, guaranteed the equal representation of the three communities (Glenny, 1996: 141).

It was precisely this principle that started to become hopelessly compromised when Bosnia had its first multi-party elections in 1990, as a response to the ever deepening Yugoslav crisis, and the three winning parties, neatly organised along national lines, were forced into a democratic coalition government. The seeds of discontent were further sowed in the autumn of 1991 when the Serbs, no doubt fearful of what happened when Croatia declared independence in 1990 and took with it a significant Serb minority of more than half-a-million, held a plebiscite that led to Serbian MP's abandoning the Sarajevo parliament and setting up their own rival parliament inside Bosnia (Glenny, 1996: 165). In this sense, the stage was already set for a confrontation, and when the Muslims and Croats of Bosnia voted for independence on 1st of March 1991 referendum, they did so with full opposition from the Bosnian Serbs, who wanted nothing more since the "Second World War [than] to be constitutionally attached to Serbia proper" (Glenny, 1996: 166). In short, the Serbs wanted, and expressed their intention to do anything in order to "ensure that they would not be a minority in a state they perceived to be hostile" (Boyd, 1995: 25). Of course this intention could never be accomplished autonomously, which helps highlight the orchestrated character of this conflict. In the words of Radovan Karadzic, then president of Republika Srpska and one of the world's most wanted war-crimes suspect: "Without Serbia, nothing would have happened, we don't have the resources and we would not have been able to make war" (HRW, 2006: 19).

If the situation described above, in extremely summarized form, seems even remotely messy - and we didn't even address the role of Croatia, who alternated between siding with the Bosnian Muslims and waging its own war on them - then this author has succeeded at giving the reader an important hint at the enormous task presented to the British news media. On the one hand, they were confronted with an extremely delicate conflict, with political ramifications that were almost Byzantine in their intricacy; on the other, they needed to present this very same conflict in an accessible and attractive manner to their home audience, who in most cases new little to nothing about these countries, about to embark in one of Europe's bloodiest wars. But it is hoped the author has also managed to hint at the consequences which a discursive practice based around the use of the Holocaust analogy might have had.

The Holocaust was an almost unimaginable crime perpetrated by the Nazi Germans against six million European Jews; it was a racially motivated crime destined to wipe out an entire ethnic minority; it was systematically planned and ruthlessly carried out through industrial scale executions; there was a clear aggressor and an undisputed victim, that didn't fight back even to save itself. The Bosnian conflict of 1992-1995 was a war of secession that involved two main military protagonists, the Bosnian Serbs and the Bosnian Muslims; at least a hundred thousand people died, two thirds of whom were Bosnian Muslims (Simons, 2007: n.p); there were reports of atrocities committed by all sides of the war, though the Bosnian Serbs have surely committed the bigger part of them; the Serb's atrocious 'ethnic cleansing' strategy had territorial objectives, not just racial ones; and in the end, the World Court has found that there was no evidence to support the claim that Serbia and the Bosnian Serbs had organized a 'Final Solution' type of strategy for the Bosnian Muslims, even though there was at least one act of genocide in Srebrenica.

In order to successfully ascertain the implications of using the Holocaust analogy in the journalistic coverage of the Bosnian conflict, this dissertation will thus be divided into five parts, notwithstanding this introduction:

- A theoretical framework, where we address the authors that deal directly with the theoretical implications of the use of the Holocaust analogy, as well as those works that deal with its larger implications as a discursive and representational practice.
- A methodological chapter, which will detail this dissertation's case study, and present our methodological tools, mostly revolving around critical linguistics and critical discourse analysis.
- An empirical analysis chapter, where *The Guardian* and the *Daily Mail* are analysed in two distinct weeks of this three year conflict – August 7th-14th 1992 and July 13th-20th 1995 – to ascertain just how 'Holocaustized' the reporting of the conflict was, and what is the nature of this 'Holocaustization'.
- A concluding chapter, where we confirm that the majority of the coverage analysed did resort to the Holocaust analogy, and where we relate our findings to our previous theoretical discussion.
- An afterword, where the lessons from this dissertation are discussed, including the problems faced along the way, what other avenues could have been explored and, also, how, if in any way, does this dissertation contribute to the wider field of media studies, in particular to the area of news discourse analysis.

***

Chapter 1 - Theorizing the Bosnian coverage

In order to achieve what I have explained above in our introductory section I have decided to divide this chapter into two distinct but interrelated subchapters. The first, called *'Holocaustizing' Bosnia*, will present a discussion revolving around the theoretical implications of using the Holocaust analogy in the journalistic coverage of the Bosnian war: which authors have dealt with the subject, what ideas they have presented, and which questions can be raised regarding the implications of this practice. The second sub-chapter, entitled *The Limits of Representation*, will contextualize this practice in the larger discussion concerning the constraints of language as a representational practice and the characteristics of discourse – and in particular, of journalistic language and discourse. It is hoped that, at the end of this chapter, the author has been successful in tracing an arc that starts with the reasons behind the usage of the Holocaust analogy and finishes with its implications as a discursive practice.

1.1 'Holocaustizing' Bosnia

> *"Would there have been such a furor over the war in Bosnia in early August 1992, if New York Newsday had not used the phrase 'death camps' in its front-page headline? Maybe not."* Charles Lane, Newsweek writer.

David Bruce MacDonald (2002), in his book, *Balkan Holocausts?*, presents a stimulating discussion between the various schools of thought surrounding the universalization of the Holocaust that serves as the perfect introduction to this chapter, and as such, is worth reproducing in some length. Starting with the idea that the Holocaust was a tragedy of such immense proportions that it "could not be applicable simply to the Jewish people" (MacDonald, 2002: 43), the author describes the efforts of those who sought to universalise its meanings, either by presenting some of its protagonists as mythological symbols of evil – such as equating Hitler with the Devil or Nazi death camps with Hell on earth – or by trying to extract general lessons from the victims' experiences, stating that the Holocaust constituted a "window into an aspect of the unarticulated but universal experience of victimization" and as such, could serve as a "bridge towards the creation of 'a new global community based on human shared values'" (Chicago cited in MacDonald, 2002: 46). Concomitantly, those who caution against universalising the Holocaust cite the dangers of generalising what they consider to be an inextricably Jewish experience; the problems of reducing the Holocaust to a "few majestic words, *Auschwitz, Holocaust,* the *Six Million*" (Finkilkraut cited in MacDonald, 2002: 46) and how this opens the door to trivialization and, in a sense, also to revisionism; and the "hijacking" (Landau cited in MacDonald, 2002: 48) of the Holocaust by minority groups eager to construct their identities and portray their suffering as *the* ultimate tragedy. MacDonald (2002) also presents a rather sophisticated, though arguably less pertinent discussion, in the context of this dissertation, revolving around the 'uniqueness' of the Holocaust and the pitfalls into which 'comparative genocidalists' might fall when using the Holocaust as the ultimate measure for tragedy (MacDonald, 2002: 49 – 51).

In her article about the implications of using the Holocaust analogy, *To Suffer by Comparison* (1999), Samantha Powers presents an anecdotal, but powerful, example of the possible effects of this practice. Recounting the efforts of a group of American Jews called "Jews against genocide" (JAG), who banded together to try and raise public awareness to what they then perceived to be the undergoing genocide in Bosnia, the author shows how the association tirelessly tried to expose the public to the horrors of Bosnia. Rallies were organised, candle-lit vigils were staged, and even a march to the Manhattan house of then UN Secretary-General Boutros Boutros-Ghali was done for the cause of awakening consciousnesses. It was all for naught. Until one day, "volunteers began shouting, 'You've seen Schindler's List; now look at Bosnia.' Suddenly, pedestrians responded, taking leaflets and stopping to inquire about events. 'We felt vulgar using the analogy,' Stone [the president of JAG] recalls, 'but it worked'" (Powers, 1999: 31).

With this very simple but powerful example Powers succeeds in highlighting one of the reasons behind the use of the Holocaust analogy, or 'Holocaustizing' (Powers, 1999: 33), as the author calls it: to grab the audience's attention, even if the method is crude. According to the author, 'Holocaustizing' is not always employed with this premeditated intention. Sometimes, journalists or advocates actively believe that the atrocities they are witnessing merit comparison with the horrors perpetrated by the Nazis. Whatever the intention, it does not seem to detract much from the final impact of the analogy. On the positive side, Powers (1999: 50) shows how the comparison *does* draw attention to previously ignored situations – *Newsday's* first article on Bosnian detention camps drew little attention until the editors headlined the second story 'THE DEATH CAMPS OF BOSNIA' – and may even effect some changes – the camps were ultimately closed shortly afterwards in a flurry of world condemnation. It may also succeed in guaranteeing that the perpetrators of modern genocide will not go unpunished, as the creation of the international courts for Rwanda and the ex-Yugoslavia demonstrate (Powers, 1999: 51). However, if the ultimate goal is to stop an ongoing genocide, then the author argues that 'Holocaustizing' is just not enough.

One of the problems with employing this particular historical analogy is that it's been overused and abused so often that it may loose most of its impact; or it may prompt other historical analogies to neutralize it in a "senseless game of tit-for-tat" (Powers, 1999: 54), such as when President Bush warned about the dangers of military intervention in Bosnia by raising the spectre of the Vietnam war. Another common criticism concerns the misrepresentation of the facts on the ground, since the Bosnian Muslims, unlike the Jews, actually confronted the Bosnian Serbs militarily and were known to have perpetrated, albeit in a much smaller scale, some of the same excesses (Powers, 1999: 54). Powers also warns that 'Holocaustizing' a particular genocide runs the risk of setting the threshold for intervention too high, with the end result of minimizing the importance of what is actually happening. Referring to Bosnia, the author argues how other atrocities perpetrated by the Serbs did not prompt such a concerted international campaign, partly because some of the factors – "a coincidence of geography and chilling set of television images" (Powers, 1999: 34) – could not be reproduced. In the end, the author concludes that the drawbacks of the Holocaust analogy far outweigh its benefits, and that 'Holocaustizing' may not be the best way to humanize a story, and is certainly not the best way to prompt outside intervention in a conflict[1].

Michael C. Desch (2006), in his essay about the use and abuse of the Holocaust analogy, takes off where Powers finishes and discusses another important reason behind

[1] For an in-depth exploration of this issue, see Powers' Pulitzer Prize wining book: *"A Problem from Hell": America and the Age of Genocide*.

the use of this historical comparison: the use of the Holocaust as a call to arms. As the author neatly explains, "the received wisdom about the Holocaust [...] is that the United States and the rest of the civilised world turned away Jews seeking to escape Nazi Germany [...] and then sat idly by while the Third Reich murdered nearly 6 million of them during the course of the war" (Desch, 2006: 107). As a consequence, they now have the moral responsibility to intervene and stop *any* ongoing genocide. In Desch's (2006) opinion, historical comparisons usually shape states' behaviour for the worse: "First, many past events are simply not related to contemporary policies. Second, decision makers tend to learn only superficial lessons from history. [...] Third, decision makers rarely consider a range of possible analogies, preferring instead to find just one. [...] Fourth, historical analogies often evoke powerful emotions like fear or guilt [...] rarely conducive to reasoned judgement" (Desch, 2006: 10-11).

Unlike Powers (1999) though, Desch considers that the Holocaust analogy, and its central tenet of 'never again', *did* significantly shape American policy towards the former Yugoslavia, leading to two military interventions: a slower one in Bosnia, and a quicker one in Kosovo. One of the main problems the author has with the use of the Holocaust analogy is that its main core – that the Allies stood by and watched instead of preventing the Jewish massacre – is based on questionable history. Desch (2006) goes on to deconstruct what he argues are some of the central myths surrounding this belief: the fact that immigration quotas prevented the salvation of many Jews; that the Allies could have bombed Auschwitz to stop the exterminations; or that Pope Pius XII did not do more to prevent the Final Solution because he was an anti-Semite. Most of all, the author opposes the use of the Holocaust analogy not only because of its faulty history, but mainly because of its politicised use. In the case of Bosnia, Desch argues that the whole Holocaust framework encouraged the Bosnian Muslims to militarily provoke the Bosnian Serbs in order to encourage NATO retaliation, an issue explored in-depth by Philip Corwin (1999). It also highlighted "superficial issues (like the colour of the victims' skin and how they were killed), instead of substantive issues (how many people were dying)" (Desch, 2006: 136).

According to the author, much of the success of this analogy in Bosnia "was due to the fact that Serb treatment of the European-appearing Muslims consisted of historically resonant actions such as putting them on trains and shipping them to concentration camps" (Desch, 2006: 136). This obfuscates the facts on the ground, prevents conflicts from being judged on their own merits, and obscures the limits of what can be done to solve them.

David Campbell (2002a, 2002b), in his sprawling two part essay about imaging the concentration camps in Bosnia tackles the issue of misrepresenting the facts head on by analysing and discussing the libel case of ITN versus *Living Marxism*. The lawsuit, filed by ITN news, targeted the highly politicised *Living Marxism* magazine – who in 1997 accused ITN reporters of fabricating the world-famous 1992 picture of emaciated Fikret Alic standing behind barbed wire in the Serb detention camp of Trnopolje. In this context, Campbell (2002b) discusses the appropriateness of these analogies while, at the same time, suggesting that *Living Marxism*'s ultimate goal was to deny that atrocities took place in Trnopolje, effectively rewriting history. While there are many interesting connotations to this argument – not the least of which is that, in the context of such an historically charged discussion, accusing *LM* of rewriting history conjures uncanny parallels to Holocaust denying – we will try, inasmuch as possible, to stay focused on the issue of misrepresentation and the implications of 'Holocaustizing' the Serb camps.

One of the most interesting questions raised by the author is the aptness of the concentration camp terminology subsequently used to describe the Serb camps. While highlighting the historical roots of the term 'concentration camp' and criticizing *LM*'s narrow view that using this term does not automatically equate the designated camp to a Nazi style extermination camp - like Auschwitz - Campbell readily admits that this term became indelibly linked to the Nazi camps. However, he then goes on to state that a comparison between Trnopolje and "Nazi style camps" is not wholly inappropriate, given that the Nazi concentration camp system was a complex system, the totality of which cannot be reduced to extermination camps like Auschwitz or Bergen-Belsen (Campbell, 2002b: 152). While this is undeniably true, there is a problematic side to it: namely, that, for better or worse, places like Auschwitz and Bergen-Belsen arguably *became* the ultimate symbol of concentration camp-evil, and that when one speaks of Nazi-style concentration camps Auschwitz is, again debatably, the first example that pops into the audience's mind because of the unspeakable atrocities committed there.

While it is true that there *were* many elements in common between Bosnian-Serb concentration camps and Nazi-concentration camps, Campbell's (2002b) argument might prove disingenuous for two reasons: Firstly, it implies that the general audience's knowledge of the Nazi-concentration camp system (not to mention of the historical origins of the term 'concentration camp') is relatively thorough. Meaning, that the majority of the audience would actively know that the Nazi concentration camp system was a complex system, where concentration camps and extermination camps coexisted, and that the latter should be seen as part, and not the totality, of this larger system. And secondly, it obscures the fact that when one employs the term 'concentration camp', the audience will have these distinctions sufficiently present so that they won't immediately associate the term with places like Auschwitz, which technically became an extermination camp, and as such, not representative of the totality of this system[2].

Admitting that the above line of argumentation is invested with some logical validity then one again has to pause and wonder if the author is not being disingenuous when stating that the Bosnian-Serb system of concentration camps is not entirely different from the Nazi one. The point is not that Campbell (2002b: 154) is wrong – he isn't, and there are common aspects between the function of the camps in the Bosnian-Serbs' ethnic cleansing strategy and the Nazi's – but rather that, implied in the context of a journalistic report, such a comparison might legitimately lead to a broader comparison between both regimes' ethnic cleansing strategies - and that might immediately point to the 'worst excesses' of the Nazi regime and its policies of industrialized, large scale mass extermination, as is ultimately symbolized by Auschwitz. Again, it seems unlikely that a general audience would filter this comparison selectively, meaning, that only the relevant points of both policies would be compared with due care for their differences.

Tackling the issue of the effects of the general public's exposure to powerful images from war torn zones and the consequences of the media's simplified coverage of complex international conflicts, Susan D. Moeller (1999a) introduced her controversial thesis of compassion fatigue. That is to say, when the media effectively 'bombards' its

[2] Much the same can be said about the term 'swastika'. While it "derives from the Sanskrit svasti + ka, meaning a mystical cross used to denote good luck" and can be "found in ancient Hindu, Mexican, Buddhist, and other traditions, possibly representing the Sun, it is now politically and culturally tainted since its appropriation by the Nazi Party as its official emblem" (Crystal Reference Encyclopedia)

audience with a daily stream of violent, emotionally-charged images, the people might respond by losing interest in whatever is being reported due to emotional exhaustion, or an overwhelming feeling that they are powerless to change the horrors to which they are continually being exposed to. Interestingly, the author also indicates that if the threshold of violence has been raised very high, but is then not adequately sustained, the public might also loose interest in what is being reported. In her portrayal of how the media covered the Bosnian conflict, Moeller (1999a) considers that the famous ITN images of Serbian concentration camps were pivotal in 'Holocaustizing' the ensuing coverage. Media critic Frederick Baker aptly summarized the impact of the famous pictures of Fikret Alic behind barbed wire: "It is the picture of famine, but then we see the barbed wire against his chest and it is the picture of the Holocaust and concentration camps" (Baker cited in Moeller, 1999a: 268)[3]. From then on, the author goes on to exemplify how the broadcasting of these images was swiftly followed by a flurry of articles and editorials that "unanimously referred to the Holocaust and the Nazis" (Moeller, 1999a: 272).

But what was the impact of all these Holocaust analogies in the case of the Bosnian camps? In Moeller's (1999a) opinion, the initial coverage, and its accompanying pictures, were so emotionally potent and charged – in part because of the horrifying reality they depicted and in part due to the historical shadows hanging over them – that, when the media failed to provide a steady stream of equally powerful images, the public just switched off and focused its attention on the next horrifying crisis, which at the time was conveniently unfolding in Somalia. While journalists arguably employed the comparisons with the intention of singling out the uniqueness of the horrors unfolding in Bosnia, their inability to provide a continuous flow of supporting images meant that the camps ended up being "relegated to yet one more itemized atrocity in the litany of abuses in Bosnia" (Moeller, 1999a: 259). And that brings us to a fourth major consequence of employing the Holocaust analogy in media reports: if it isn't continually sustained with powerful, iconic, images, the initial impact might quickly fade and, instead of singling out the distinctiveness of the victims'

[3] It is interesting to note, in the context of the discussion raised in analysing the Campbell (2002a, 2002b) articles, how difficult it is, nowadays, to dissociate the terms 'Holocaust' and 'concentration camps'. It seems that the term 'concentration camp' already implicitly carries around the ghost of the Holocaust, and that separating the two in the audience's mind might truly prove to be impossible, or at least extremely hard to do.

suffering it might actually diminish that suffering, by lumping it together with the other, never ending horrors of war.

In a way, Moeller's (1999a) book seems to indicate that modern audiences are so accustomed to being confronted with reports of unspeakable violence that the threshold of suffering has to be set unimaginably high to sustain their interest and force political leaders to commit to some sort of action. A consequence of this is that if the media raise the threshold of suffering by invoking the ghosts of the Holocaust, but then fail to adequately sustain the momentum by supplying its audience with a continuous stream of visual 'proof', the public might quickly loose interest. But on the other hand, if the coverage is too emotionally charged, it can also result in 'compassion fatigue', and repel the public in that way.

Dutch scholars Ruigrok, de Ridder and Scholten (2005), came to a similar conclusion in their essay on the coverage of the Bosnian war in Dutch Newspapers. Arguing that the 1992 pictures from Trnopolje set the basis for articles "full of emotional references to atrocities committed during World War II" (Ruigrok et al, 2005: 179), the authors considered that these first articles set an initial frame of coverage revolving around the victims and humanitarian intervention. However, when the continuous emphasis on human suffering succeeded in diluting the initial uniqueness of the concentration camp reports, the Dutch readers progressively started to develop Bosnia fatigue. By 1995, Dutch newspapers, sensing the tiredness of their public, had almost completely dropped the human framework, and were covering the conflict mostly through a diplomatic and international relations prism.

> Only when the gravity of human suffering [reached] a level without precedent, as during the massacre accompanying the fall of Srebrenica, [did] newspapers [again] pay attention to this theme (Ruigrok, et al 2005: 178).

But why do journalists choose to employ this analogy in the first place? Susan D. Moeller (1999b) in her study, *Four Habits of International News Reporting*, attempts to answer this question:

> Since most of the media assume the public is not interested in international news, there is a perceived need to hype the coverage of 'foreign' events to an even greater extent than domestic news (Moeller, 1999b: 1).

In this respect, Moeller (1999b) argues that when journalists are covering foreign events, and especially foreign crises, they usually lapse into four distinct habits. The first, which the author calls 'formulaic coverage', consists of a tendency to report on a specific occurrence in black and white terms, with the media so fixing a

> conception in our minds that we cannot disentangle the stereotyped characterization of a group or person from the facts. So Saddam Hussein and Slobodan Milosevic become evil, the doctors from Médecins Sans Frontières are fearless, the thousands of refugees are all victims (Moeller, 1999b: 2).

In this sense, the causes and solutions to a specific crisis are automatically simplified and the language of reporting becomes the "language of a morality play, with good and evil fighting for ascendancy, and characters fit into the parts of victim, rescuer and villain" (Moeller 199b: 2). Victims, however, must be 'pure', and not ideologically aligned with any of the sides of the conflict or in any way politicised. In fact, depoliticisation is crucial for the presentation of a conflict as an "encounter [that takes] place outside any context, as part of an eternal encounter between evil and innocence" (Mamdani, 2007, n.p.). This strategy has distinct advantages, especially when the reporting is on something as massive as genocide, as in the case of Bosnia. Firstly, it gives the moral high ground to those who report on the ongoing genocide; and secondly, and perhaps most importantly, genocide becomes part of "a rhetorical arsenal that helps you vilify your adversaries while ensuring impunity for your allies" (Mamdani, 2007, n.p.). But it is also important to note that having the moral high ground in reporting a conflict might frequently lead the reporter to righteously dismiss such important journalistic notions as impartiality or fairness to both sides. Mick Hume, the editor of the controversial *Living Marxism* magazine, which was forced to close after the ITN lawsuit, speaks about some of the consequences of this approach:

> [It] is self righteous. Worse, it is repressive. Those who fall on the wrong side of the line the press corps draws between Good and Evil [...] can expect to be on the receiving end of more than bad press (Hume cited in McLaughlin, 2002: 166).

The second habit consists of employing a stream of sensationalised, emotionally charged language revolving around dramatic words and phrases, which become the hallmark of the coverage. This invariably leads to the use of analogies, metaphors and images, a third habit which the author relates not only with sensationalism, but also with a tendency to substitute a complex reality with a knowable one. Journalists are particularly found of historical analogies. Moeller explains that comparing

> a crisis to the Holocaust is an exercise in moral equivalence; it signals to readers and viewers the scale of deaths in a crisis as well as the intent of the murderers (Moeller, 1999b: 5).

And lastly, coverage must find a way to relate the story to the audience's home country.

These four habits implicitly carry with them another practice: pack journalism. In his contribution to the Netherlands Institute for War Documentation's report on the fall of Srebrenica, Jan Wieten (2002) explains how the foreign correspondent's need to provide a constant stream of news means that

> the content of the media is [...] largely determined by what other media and other journalists consider to be important, a situation that can occasionally result in 'pack journalism' (Wieten, 2002: n.p.).

In the author's analysis, this lead to a situation where

> opinions which are not in line with [the] established view are given less opportunity to be heard, and events which do not match the overall pattern are likely to be ignored (Wieten, 2002: n.p.).

John Burns (1996), a British professor, complained about the same phenomenon regarding the media's coverage of the Yugoslav civil wars, stating that it became "almost impossible for a commentator to question the received wisdom of those around him or her" (Burns, 1996: 92). Pierre Bourdieu aptly summarizes this particular journalistic phenomenon by explaining how it is born from the obsessive regime of "permanent surveillance [...] to which journalists subject their competitors' activities" (Bourdieu, 1998: 72). In this sense, competition is perverted, and instead of "automatically generating originality and diversity [it] tends to favour *uniformity*" by incestuously producing "themes [...] that 'must' bet taken up again, [and] subjects that 'have to be covered'" (Bourdieu, 1998: 72) just because all the other media outlets are talking about them. But this practice has another powerful side-effect which we will discuss in more detail below: by aggressively stifling dissent it violently sets the boundaries of what can acceptably be said about the war in Bosnia.

1.2 The limits of representation

Public representations have the power to select, arrange, and prioritize certain assumptions and ideas about different kinds of people, bringing some to the fore [...] while casting others into social margins – Michael Pickering

Of course, one of the things we have been hinting at in the above discussion regarding the implications of using the Holocaust analogy in the context of the Bosnian conflict concerns the way in which it affected and helped construct the journalistic discourse about this particular Balkan war. Discourse is a controversial and highly slippery notion and trying to find one single definition might prove as fruitless as it is Herculean. However, one can tentatively affirm that at least one of its constituent parts has to do with setting the limits about what can be said concerning a particular subject or field. To put it in other words:

> it governs the way that a topic can be meaningfully talked about and reasoned about [and] influences how ideas are put into practices and used to regulate the conduct of others (Hall, 1997: 44).

If the shadow of Michel Foucault hangs heavy on this last statement it is because it is almost impossible for latter-day works on discourse to escape reference to the work of the French philosopher. In fact, Foucault introduced a series of revolutionary, if radical, changes to the field of discourse analysis that are worth mentioning, albeit in a crudely summarized manner. The first of these changes concerns the thorough 'historicization' of *any* discourse, which means that any knowledge and 'truth' produced by it is inextricably bound to "a specific historical context" (Hall, 1997: 46). Secondly, knowledge and its associated discursive practices are intimately related to the exercise of power, and not only in the above mentioned regulatory sense. This brings us to a third proposition: "Knowledge linked to power, not only assumes the authority of 'the truth' but has the power to *make itself true*" (Foucault cited in Hall 1997: 49). That is to say, 'truth' is produced in a war-like context by power and is in this way imposed on us: taken to its logical extreme, 'truth' does not have any continuous, outside existence: it is always produced and bound to a certain historical period.

The idea of knowledge – and 'truth' – as the by-products of a war-like confrontation between various parties has been brilliantly explored by Eduard Said in his seminal work, *Covering Islam*, on the role of the media in shaping our perceptions of the Islamic world. In it, Said introduces the helpful notion of 'communities of interpretation', which can be loosely defined as the different parties (with different interests, different cultural backgrounds and different degrees of power) which intervene and compete in the production of knowledge about a given subject.

> In other words, what we are dealing with here are in the very widest sense communities of interpretation, many of them at odds with one another, prepared in many instances literally to go to war with one another (Said, 1997: 45)

over what they consider to be their 'true' interpretation of a given phenomenon. The Western media are, in this sense, a collection of particularly powerful 'communities of interpretation' with immense resources to forcefully impose their specific 'truth' about a given topic. In this sense, and considering the pack journalism that ensued in Bosnia (Burns 1996, Wieten 2002), it is not difficult to comprehend how 'the Holocaust analogy might have been aggressively imposed by the media as the undisputed way to represent the conflict.

The media are also especially well positioned to exercise what Pierre Bourdieu called 'symbolic power'. Symbolic power is part of a triad of definitions, developed through a lifetime of work, including symbolic capital and symbolic violence[4], which we will try to define here, although in admittedly oversimplified terms. Simply put, symbolic power is the "power of 'worldmaking' [of] carrying out a decomposition, an analysis, and a composition, a synthesis, often by the use of labels" (Bourdieu, 1989: 22). It is also the power "to designate or to describe individuals, groups or institutions"

[4] The notion of symbolic capital is fully developed in, among other works, *Distinction*: *A Social Critique of Judgement of Taste*, while one of the clearest definitions of symbolic violence can be found in the *Logic of Practice*.

(Bourdieu, 1989: 23). To exercise it, one has to be invested with a certain amount of symbolic capital, that is to say, one has to possess that which can be "recognized as legitimate competence, as authority" (Bourdieu, 1983: 6). Finally, symbolic power often takes the form of symbolic violence, a subtle, non-physical, form of coercion that acts invisibly, or at least goes unrecognized by those who suffer it, but which seeks to alter their actions or their worldview on a certain topic. According to the author, the media exercise an especially potent brand of symbolic violence. Television journalism, in particular, is the main culprit, violently imposing its worldview through its unprecedented power to reach a massive amount of people; by effectively monopolizing who has access to the public space; by forcing issues to fit television's structural necessities[5] (Bourdieu 1998); and, perhaps most importantly, regarding Bosnia, by being recognized by the public as the legitimate authority to produce knowledge on the war.

Again, it is not hard to see how the use of the Holocaust analogy fits into Bourdieu's concepts. For a start, it gives the user the moral high ground, investing them with a certain amount of 'symbolic capital' which can be employed, if need be violently, to silence the opposition and fix discursive boundaries – what can be called, in its most extreme form, the "self-righteous use of the Holocaust as 'symbolic capital'" (LaCapra cited in Friedlander, 1992: 112). After all, nobody wants to be labelled as the equivalent of a Holocaust denier. And it is also not hard to guess what Bourdieu might have commented on the way in which the famous ITN pictures conditioned a significant part of the journalistic framework on the Bosnian war.

In a way, Bourdieu's concern with the constraining structural dictates of television news encapsulates the importance of analysing the peculiarities of journalistic discourse in general. The main reason for this is that,

> as readers of newspapers, and viewers of television, we readily assume that the *Nine O' Clock News*, or the front page of the *Daily Express* or *The Guardian*, consists of faithful reports that happened 'out there', in the world beyond our immediate experience (Fowler, 1991: 10-11),

[5] Structural necessities which, according to Bourdieu (1998) but also to Neil Postman (1985), hopelessly simplify, emotionalize and package information, politics, and other vital components of democratic citizenship into something always entertaining.

effectively legitimizing them as 'truthful'. This 'taking for granted' happens precisely because "people are not in general trained to see through the veils of media representations" (Fowler, 1991: 11). As such, the ideas of news as a manufactured commodity, of language as inextricably value-laden, or of news-values not so much as categories of selection but mostly as categories of representation are likely to be alien to the average newsreader. However, this does not diminish their importance in the context of the discourse of journalism.

Take the use of stereotypes. While it is commonly accepted that journalists usually resort to stereotypes in the course of their work, the implications of this representational practice are frequently unaccounted for. For example, while it is commonly accepted that stereotypes function as a restrictive practice, they are not always seen as inflexible structures, deeply related to questions of order and power, and essential to the maintenance of a certain *status quo* (Pickering, 2001: 3). That they do this by creating an "illusion of precision in defining and evaluating other people" and that "those who are stereotyped [...] are then fixed into a marginal position [...] and judged accordingly, regardless of the inaccuracies that are involved in the stereotypical description given of them" (Pickering, 2001: 4-5). Or that their contradiction with complex and precise information is not always enough to dissipate them, a process which is usually only accomplished by the passage of time, since stereotypes are deeply historicized. That means that, in the case of the journalistic coverage of Bosnia, 'Holocaustizing' – and its implied stereotypes of the Serbs as Nazis and the Bosnian Muslims as Jews –almost certainly imposed a rigid structure which did not allow for significant deviations - such as stories about atrocities committed by Muslims or reports of Serb suffering – and might have perpetuated misrepresentations that may only be dissipated in another historical context.

Of course, not everything is negative concerning the use of these representational practices. On a more positive note, the use of symbolism or stereotypes can quickly provide a peg that will make an unfamiliar situation understandable to a large segment of the audience.

1.3 Conclusion

Now that we have succeeded in presenting this dissertation's general theoretical framework it is perhaps appropriate to review some of the main points that can be extracted from this discussion, and tie them to this dissertation's overall arguments. There are a number of important conclusions which can be summarized from the above presentation. Firstly, that the Holocaust analogy is used as a method, albeit a crude one, to attract attention; secondly, that 'Holocaustizing' a conflict is an effective way to righteously appeal for outside military intervention; thirdly, that the Holocaust analogy can misrepresent the facts on the ground, creating powerful and constrictive stereotypes that may condition the discourse on a certain subject for an extended amount of time, even when contradicted with alternative information; fourthly, that it may actually 'fatigue' the public when it is not continually sustained by powerful visual 'proof'; fifthly, that it serves as a potent simplifying process that thoroughly depoliticises the reported conflict; and sixthly, that it can function as a powerful "rhetoric arsenal" (Mamdani, 2007: n.p) which gives the media a substantial amount of 'symbolic capital' that it can use to its advantage in the interpretative struggle to establish the 'truth' of what happened and to determine the limits of what can be said about a certain subject.

In this sense, it is important to note that 'Holocaustizing' is very much a part of the media's discourse on war, and that it is born, sustained, and imposed, by the habits and processes of the journalistic profession. That is to say, if discourses always produce deeply historicized 'truths' that operate within the boundaries erected by both the statements that are considered valid and the extra-discursive practices that frame them, then 'Holocaustizing', as a discursive strategy, is very much the result of the collision between a certain 'historicized' reality and the practices and constraints of the journalistic profession. Meaning, that many of the above-mentioned aspects of the journalistic practice – such as formulaic coverage, simplification or pack journalism – actually combine with the language used in these journalistic reports to establish and reinforce discursive strategies like 'Holocaustizing'. In this respect, the use of the Holocaust analogy does not fix discursive boundaries only because of its historical potency but also because it is born and perpetuated by the functional practices of the journalistic profession.

So where does this dissertation fit in regard to the above discussion? In many ways, it proposes to investigate several of these points, though it is not exclusively bound to any of these particular theories. In this sense, it also agrees that 'Holocaustizing' is a powerful simplifying procedure that has the potential to offer not only a restrictive interpretation of the situation on the ground but, more importantly, to fix the boundaries of accepted discourse for an indeterminate amount of time. However, this author is particularly interested in investigating *how* this is done, and what are the processes involved. For instance, how does the journalist apply the Holocaust's morally undisputed categories of extreme 'Evil' versus defenceless 'Good', to a situation of civil war? How does this discursive strategy deal with morally complex information? And in what way does the use of the Holocaust analogy carry with it an underlying ideology, as suggested in the above discussion?

In this respect, I very much agree that behind the use of the Holocaust analogy lie many ideologies: a bellicose ideology; an ideology of humanitarian compassion; perhaps even a slightly condescending ideological superiority where 'We' should intervene to stop the barbarity of the uncivilized 'Other'. This is certainly one of the main aspects which we will investigate in our empirical analysis of the journalistic coverage. But in order to do this, this dissertation's methodology will now be described.

Chapter 2 - Methodology

"I would like my books to be a kind of tool-box which others can rummage through to find a tool which they can use however they wish in their own area." Michel Foucault

In order to adequately respond to our research question we have chosen to analyse two British Newspapers – *The Guardian* and *The Daily Mail* – in two distinct, one week, periods of the Bosnian war. The first period, comprising the week of August 7th to August 14th, is the week when ITN broadcast its famous pictures of emaciated Fikret Alic and the detention camps of Omarska and Trnopolje, which were subsequently accompanied by a flurry of newspaper articles detailing conditions inside these detention camps and discussing how they fit into the Bosnian Serb's war strategy. The second time period refers to the week of July 13th to July 20th, which starts with the day the UN safe area of Srebrenica was captured by the Serb paramilitary army of general Radko Mladic and continues with the subsequent speculation of what was happening to the thousands of Muslim men and boys that 'disappeared' from the enclave. Why these two particular newspapers, and why these two specific weeks in this three year conflict? Perhaps it is easier to start this answer by first addressing the time period.

As the astute reader has no doubt noticed, these two weeks are some of the most newsworthy and explosive weeks of the entire conflict and are some of the most appropriate for the subject matter being investigated by this dissertation. In this sense, they were chosen not only because of the violent and tragic events they depicted, or their inherent newsworthiness, but, above all, because of how adequate they might be in answering this dissertation's research question. The period relating to August 1992 was absolutely crucial in determining a large part of the journalistic framework regarding the war: in this respect, it was felt that it was essential to analyze at least this more conclusive part of a summer rife with rumours about the Bosnian Serb's war atrocities and uncertainties regarding just what the Serbs meant by 'ethnic cleansing'. It was also the most historically resonant face of a barbarous strategy, which explains why this week will be analyzed instead of any of the equally atrocious weeks of the Sarajevo siege – which is still arguably the most potent symbol of the Bosnian conflict. The first week of the Srebrenica events was chosen not only because of the historical resonance of the episode but, mainly, because of the uncertainty surrounding what had actually happened at the time. While it is now common to hear or read about Srebrenica as 'Europe's worst massacre since World War II', things were not so clear-cut in the immediate aftermath of the event - which makes analysing this first week especially interesting in the context of this dissertation.

However, there were alternative time periods that could have yielded equally interesting information - the countless weeks of journalistic coverage of the many trials at the ICTY being the most obvious example. The author is also aware that the time periods chosen constitute especially 'hot' weeks in the journalistic coverage of this conflict and, in this sense, might seem conveniently hand-picked to answer this dissertation's research question. While I am aware of the possibility of this latter criticism, I can only counter that, in the context and time frame of this MA Dissertation, I did not hesitate to choose journalistic moments that, because of the events they depicted, might, at least in theory, be more conducive to this project's central research question. However, this is also a bit of gamble, because if these two time periods do not yield conclusive information about the use of the Holocaust analogy, then 'Holocaustizing' might not be such a useful way to analyse the journalistic coverage of the Bosnian conflict.

This brings me to another problem the reader might have with this dissertation's approach: the lack of a sustained analysis. In fact, centring an analysis on just two, out of more than a hundred and fifty-five available weeks of journalistic coverage on this war might prompt some to question just what can be extracted out of such a small and discontinuous sample. Again, I can only answer that the lack of a more sustained approach is due to the material and time constraints of this academic project, and that the conclusions extracted at the end of this analysis should be interpreted bearing in mind the specific constraints that produced them.

This also applies to the choice of newspapers. Why *The Guardian* and *The Daily Mail*? In fact, why choose two British newspapers to serve as representatives of the international journalistic coverage of this conflict? There are several reasons for this. The first has to do with the fact that British newspapers were at the forefront in reporting and championing certain events and views on this war. *The Guardian*'s Ed Vuliamy, for example, accompanied ITN and Channel Four's reporters on their visit to the detention camps of Omarska and Trnopolje, and his reports were essential in exposing the appalling conditions inside Serb detention camps. But he was not the only one: Maggie O' Keane, another famous name in the context of this war, was also a *Guardian* reporter at this time. On the other hand, *The Daily Mirror* and *The Daily Mail* were quick to frame ITN's pictures as 'proof' of the Serbs' Nazi-like intentions, and were instrumental in suggesting how this conflict should be read. But most importantly, Britain was one of the key European countries in the debate for military intervention in Bosnia, besides being one of the two largest contributors – the other one was France – to the United Nations Protection Force (UNPROFR), a peacekeeping force operating in Bosnia at the time. As such, analyzing the way in which the British media framed the war is indispensable to comprehending what were the media's desires regarding the future direction of British foreign policy at this important moment in European history.

However, the author is again aware that there were equally interesting alternatives. The Dutch press, for instance, would have been extremely interesting to analyze - if this author had the requisite language skills - especially because of the Dutch involvement in the Srebrenica massacre and their overall desire to commit troops to Bosnia. And the American press, from this point of view, might have yielded similarly revealing results, since there was enormous pressure on the Bush and Clinton administrations to militarily intervene in Bosnia. Trans-national media comparisons might have been an option in a different project, but were immediately discarded for fear that they would make the sample analysed even more discontinuous.

In this sense, *The Guardian* and *The Daily Mail* were chosen precisely to illustrate some difference while, at the same time, providing some national coherence to this analysis. Founded in 1821 by businessman John Edward Taylor under the title *Manchester Guardian,* the newspaper changed its name to *The Guardian* in 1959. With a circulation of more than 370 000 copies per day and a readership of 1 263 000 people[6], *The Guardian* is a liberal newspaper known for it's left of centre inclination and is a formal supporter of the Liberal Party of Britain. It is also famous for taking up

[6] For more information, refer to: http://adinfo-guardian.co.uk/the-guardian/guardian-circulation-and-readership.shtml

'worthy causes' in its reports and for being read by those who plan to run Britain. *The Daily Mail* was Britain's premiere daily newspaper, first published in 1896, and is the country's best-selling newspaper after *The Sun*, with a circulation of almost two and a half million copies and six million readers[7]. It is not considered a tabloid anymore, but rather, a middle-market newspaper, of conservative orientation, that might be seen, in many ways, as the voice of middle-England. As such, it can also be seen as the antithesis of *The Guardian*, since it tends to be ideologically allergic to immigrants, the European Union, and abortion - to list some of the themes that have been regularly defended by the liberal newspaper.

As the reader will have no doubt noticed by now, there are no tabloids included in this sample. This might seem strange, since the tabloids should be an obvious target, given their penchant for bombastic language. However, this author is convinced that 'Holocaustizing' was so widespread that one can find evidence of it in all the newspapers, regardless of their quality.

Having introduced and explained the rationale behind our sample choice, it is time to describe it in detail and expound further on this dissertation's methodology. Regarding our sample (see Table 1, bellow), it is comprised of a total of 126 articles divided into two broad categories: 'Reports' and 'Editorials'. The idea behind this division is not so much to create two new artificial categories but, rather, to try and reproduce a division that is very much present in the pages of most modern newspapers: the division between so-called factual articles, written by the newspapers' staff reporters, and the more opinionated editorials or features written by selected journalists and other relevant figures of a given society, such as historians or politicians.

In this sense, the 'Reports' category consists of what one could call a more traditional news piece, dedicated to exposing the readers to events that "happened 'out there', in the world beyond [their] immediate experience" (Fowler, 1991: 11). This includes human interest stories, 'breaking news' stories, political stories, or any other report dedicated to informing the public about something 'new'. It also includes those reports where the factual content clearly surpasses any subjective interpretation, and where the writer does not directly invest the stories with an obvious predisposition.

[7] For detailed figures, refer to: http://www.associatednewspapers.com/dailymail.htm

The 'Editorials' category, on the other hand, will take in all the other articles that in some way contain the author's *a posteriori* point of view on a certain event. This means that editorials, op-eds, leading articles and all other such analytical pieces will be included in this category. Obviously, the author is well aware of the artificiality of this division and its problematic nature, even in the day-to-day life of newspapers, since there are articles that clearly defy both, some of which we have also encountered in this sample. Unfortunately, it is impossible, in the context of this dissertation, to create a more detailed third category that would more accurately reflect this complexity.

Having said that, the majority of our sample falls into the 'Reports' category, with a total of 98 such articles, against a sum of 28 'Editorials'.

Table 1

The Guardian/ Daily Mail	Reports	Editorials	**Total**
August 7th – 14th	**59**	**16**	**75**
July 13th – 20th	**39**	**12**	**51**
Total	**98**	**28**	**126**

It is also important to mention that our sample is entirely made up of online versions of the original newspaper articles culled from the Lexis Nexis Professional Database. In this sense, they are purely textual versions, devoid of any graphical representations, and detached from their original position in the newspaper, though there are indicators that help give the reader some hints regarding these two latter points. Still, this author is aware that there are important differences between doing an analysis in possession of the original newspaper articles and analysing their online, textual versions. The most obvious one is that the strict textual nature of the online versions will automatically condition this dissertation's methodological tools, which will revolve around critical linguistics and critical discourse analysis. In this sense, the richness of a semiotic approach is lost on this sample, and important clues to interpreting these articles – such as their place in the newspaper page, the pictures that accompany them, the font size of the headlines, or the article's intertextual relation with the other features on the same page – will be absent. An obvious question at this point would be: why not use the original versions then? Again, practical constraints dictate the answer. The reality is that it is much more convenient and much less time consuming to cull these articles from the Lexis Nexis Database – where they are available for consultation at any time of the day, are easy to search, and can be inexpensively printed if needed – than to photocopy 126 articles which are only available at select libraries. In this sense, a compromise between what the articles might divulge and the easiness in obtaining them was reached in the context and time-frame of this dissertation. Having said that, a purely textual analysis can still divulge an immensity of information, as some of the authors presented bellow will detail.

Taking as his starting point the premise that "representation [...] is patterned by the structure of the medium" Roger Fowler applies critical linguistics to

> "the minute details of [a text's] linguistic structure [...] to display to consciousness the patterns of belief and value which are encoded in the language – and which are below the threshold of notice for anyone who accepts the discourse as 'natural' (Fowler, 1991: 66-67).

This is done by paying close attention to how grammatical structures are employed and how they "arrange, delete and assign a role and status to elements of texts and utterances", all of this with an eye to understanding how "social meanings [are] conditioned by syntactic choices" (Deacon et al, 1998: 150). Examples of this can be found in Fowler's minute examination of how journalistic texts 'nominalise' and 'passivise' language - and what are the implications of this. 'Nominalisation' – the process of making a noun out of other words, such as verbs or adjectives – is seen as a way to de-subjectify actions, of obfuscating agency, and of objectifying processes; whereas 'passivisation' – turning verbs into their passive form – can delete agency to protect certain interest groups by hiding their negative actions (Deacon et al., 1998: 150-151). But Fowler is also interested in analysing how "vocabulary [represents] the world as perceived according to the ideological needs of a culture" (Fowler, 1991: 82). In this sense, the author observes how journalistic discourse re-labels existing phenomena or creates new words to describe something – what Fowler calls relexicalisation – to suit different cultural needs; or how journalism deploys a multiplicity of synonyms to describe things which are intensely preoccupying for certain groups – what is known as overlexicalisation. However, Fowler insists that such 'technical' analyses can never be detached from the overall context:

> In the case of newspaper discourse, this means finding out what one can about the institutional and economic structure of the newspaper industry, its political relations [...] and so on (Fowler, 1991: 90).

Expanding this idea several steps further, Norman Fairclough considers that texts are not closed entities and that meaning in texts occurs "as the interplay between the 'traces' they bear of their production and the 'cues' they provide for their interpretation", never forgetting that "productional and interpretive processes are conditioned by the situational, institutional and societal contexts in which they take place" (Deacon et al., 1998: 152).In the case of media texts this approach, called critical discourse analysis, examines how the media translate official points of view into popular language, disguising the ideological connotations of official discourse with the language of common sense. Or in other words, Fairclough observes "how official discourses [...] are articulated with colloquial discourses [...] within a genre of hard news" (Fairclough 1995, 70). This process is accomplished by the various 'cues' encoded in media texts which present this linguistic transformation to the reader as a natural phenomenon - a *fait accompli* - by blurring the lines between the different voices in the text. In one of the most interesting aspects of his critical discourse analysis theory, the author effectively demonstrates how the various discourses that constitute a journalistic text interact and are transformed from their original versions. This is only possible due to the comprehensive nature of Fairclough's tripartite method, where he first analyses a journalistic text as a communicative event – investigating how source texts are transformed in the making of a media text – followed by an analysis of how a particular text fits into a wider genre and concluding by observing the "socio-cultural practice which has framed the stabilization of this sort of discourse type" (Fairclough, 1995: 73).

Finishing with the idea that ideology is at its most effective when it is rendered invisible, it is worth quoting Fairclough on this at some length:

> Reports are rarely even-handed with all the various voices represented. Some are given prominence, and some marginalized. Some are used to frame others. Some are legitimized by being taken up in the newsreader's or reporter's voice, others are not. Equity and balance cannot be assessed by merely noting which voices are represented, and, for instance, how much space is given to each" (Fairclough, 1995: 81).

In this sense, Fairclough hints at how journalistic notions of fairness and objectivity can be used to cloak partisanship and promote certain ideological viewpoints.

Perhaps it would be useful, at this point, to further elaborate on how ideologies are transmitted by the media. Considering that the main function of ideologies "is the *co-ordination* of the social practices of group members for the effective realization of the goals of a social group, and the protection of its interests" (Van Dijk, 1998: 24), Dutch scholar Teun van Dijk investigates how they are represented by the media. In this sense, the author traces the cognitive structure of ideologies – e.g. 'Us and Them' – followed by the models that reflect them – e.g. 'Black people are less intelligent than White people' in the case of a model of racial ideology – and finishing with the transition to discourse, in the form of a text or an oral speech. Van Dijk then employs a vast and complex array of analytical tools to show how ideologies manifest themselves in media texts. While it is beyond the scope of this methodological chapter to properly cover all of them, a simplified summary of some of these techniques includes: analysing media texts for polar structures, the classic being the 'Us versus Them' structure; opinion coherence; how facts are attributed; what terms are used to describe them and how does this reflect the text's structure - e.g. 'hard' terms will almost certainly describe the actions of our enemies while 'soft' terms are likely to describe the actions of our friends, even if they are negative; implicitness or explicitness of opinion; what are the text's 'unmentionables' - e.g. negative criticisms towards the journalist's host country; and also, what are the arguments used, and how are they supported (Van Dijk, 1998: 57-61).

If the above-mentioned methods are commonly referred to as qualitative content analysis, some quantitative methods will also be employed in this account. The idea is not so much to produce an "objective, systematic, and quantitative description of the manifest content of communication" (Berelson cited in Schrøder, 2002: 103) but to complement the main qualitative analysis with some relevant statistical data.. It is also worth stating that we will not subscribe exclusively to any of the above-mentioned methodological approaches but will instead take a utilitarian approach to them, much in the style of Michel Foucault's quote at the start of this chapter. That is to say, from Fowler (1991) we plan to use concepts mainly related to how vocabulary is applied –

such as 'overlexicalisation' – and what it reveals about the writer's "attitude" towards what he is writing about – what the author calls "modality" (Fowler, 1991: 85). From Fairclough's (1995) complex method we will chiefly apply his principle of analysing how the different voices in a text combine, and how official ideology is sometimes surreptitiously transmitted by the journalist. And Van Dijk (1998) will provide us with the tools to analyse how 'Holocaustizing', as a discursive strategy, is implemented and how this affects the structure of the text.

Finally, it might be appropriate to address just what is meant by the general label of 'Holocaust analogy', and how we will search for it in our articles. In this sense, and as we have hinted in the above discussions, the articles will be scanned for terms which are in any way connected to the Holocaust. This means that terms such as 'concentration camp', 'Nazi', 'genocide', 'commandant', 'mass grave', or any other terms connected to the Holocaust will be considered, besides the word 'Holocaust' itself. We will also specify *how* the references are made, meaning, if they are direct references, i.e. in the reporter's 'voice', or indirect references attributed to any third party, and how they are interwoven in the text.

***

Chapter 3 - Empirical Findings

Having explained this dissertation's methodology it is perhaps useful to introduce the reader to our next chapter. As mentioned before, this chapter will deal with our empirical analysis of *The Guardian* and the *Daily Mail* in order to ascertain how present the Holocaust analogy was, and discuss its nature. In order to do this, we will dedicate the first part of our chapter to the week of August 7th – 14th 1992, followed by our analysis of the first week of coverage - July 13th – 20th 1995 - of the Srebrenica Massacre. In the end, some concluding remarks will tie the two analyses together and extract the relevant conclusions.

3.1 August 7th- 14th: 'Belsen 92'

Unsurprisingly, the week of the transmission of ITN's famous pictures of the detention camps of Trnopolje and Omarska produced a flurry of journalistic articles. Among *The Guardian* and the *Daily Mail* a total of 75 journalistic pieces were written between August 7th and August 14th (see Table 2 bellow). Of this total, 59 articles fall into the 'Reports' category with the remaining 16 being 'Editorial' pieces. *The Guardian* clearly takes the lead in the amount of articles written in this week of August, with a total of 59 stories, against just 16 from the *Daily Mail.* There is also a significant difference between both newspapers' 'Reports' and 'Editorials' categories, with the former registering a much higher number of articles than the latter. On average, *The Guardian* published 6.57 'Reports' articles per issue and 1.83 'Opinion' pieces, against the *Daily Mail*'s 1.86 'Reports' articles per issue and 0.43 'Opinion' pieces (a number explained by the absence of any opinion pieces in four out of the seven days analysed).

Table 2

August 7th – 14th	Reports	Editorials	**Total**

The Guardian	**46**	**13**	**59**
The Daily Mail	**13**	**3**	**16**
Total	**59**	**16**	**75**

The Guardian's edition of August 7th published a total of seven articles on Bosnia – five 'Reports' and two 'Editorial′ pieces – and is worth analysing in some detail. The newspaper opens with Ed Vulliamy's page one article on the detention camps of Omarska and Trnopolje, written after accompanying Chanel 4 and ITN's journalists to the same camps. Entitled 'Shame of Camp Omarska'[8], Vulliamy's article was crucial in exposing the appalling conditions of the Serb detention camps and as such will be the first to be analysed in the context of this dissertation's main research questions.

If one would have to summarize the main theme of Vulliamy's article one could say that it is the ideational struggle, to use Fowler's (1991) terms, on how to represent the detention camps of Omarska and Trnopolje. In fact, there is such confusion and uncertainty regarding this subject that one can clearly distinguish the traces the article bears of its production and the cues it gives to its interpretation (Fairclough, 1995). In this respect, there is no blurring of the line effect between official voices and the reporter's voice: on the contrary, they are clearly separated. Of the ten 'concentration camp' references present throughout the text, the only time it is taken up in the reporter's voice is in paragraph thirty-five with the express purpose of denying this classification to the detention centre of Trnopolje – referred to as the "second biggest 'concentration camp'" by the Muslim government three paragraphs before – based on Vulliamy's own observations of the site. The first time the term appears in the text it is clearly attributed to the Bosnian government, and from then on it is always qualified by some source other than the writer. It also usually appears between quotation marks, demonstrating Vulliamy's need to distance himself from the designation. In this sense, while the use of the Holocaust analogy is omnipresent throughout the story it does not originate with the writer: he merely reproduces it and always keeps his distance.

[8] Included as Appendix 1

In fact, the most indicative sign of 'Holocaustizing' present in this story pertains to the reason behind its writing, explained by Vulliamy on paragraph ten: an invitation to the journalists by Radovan Karadzic, then president of Republika Srpska, to inspect whatever they wanted to see in response to the concentration camp allegations made by the Bosnian government. In this sense, the writer provides the reader with various cues on how to make up his own mind about the camps, while reproducing their official categorizations. These cues are provided by Vulliamy's descriptions of the internees and his choice of vocabulary: inmates are described as 'emaciated', 'sunken-eyed', with 'spindly hands', eating 'like a famished dog', 'cadaverous', 'thin', 'raw-boned' and so on. In this sense, there is some evidence of what Fowler (1991) described as 'overlexicalisation', in this case catering to *The Guardian's* supposedly liberal and humanitarian readership.

What is happening at the Omarska camp is a 'secret', despite what the reporters were able to see, because Karadzic's invitation to visit the camp collapses midway through the tour, and the journalists were not able to inspect some parts of it. It is also shameful, as one of the Serb coordinators admits in paragraph twenty-three - and as Vulliamy corroborates in the title - and there is 'humiliation' of the prisoners, thought the journalist saw no "signs of violence or beating [...] let alone systematic extermination"[9] (Vulliamy, 1992: n.p). But in the end Vulliamy is unsure of how to categorize it, choosing the adjective 'sinister', in paragraph thirty-five, to give the reader his view of what the Serbs call an 'investigation centre' and what the Bosnian Muslims call a 'concentration camp'. In the end, it is the reader who will have to make up his mind on whether the camp is sinister enough to be considered a concentration camp.

Trnopolje, the second camp observed, is categorically denied the status of 'concentration camp' by the journalist, and is described as something "between a civilian prison and transit camp" (Vulliamy, 1992: n.p.). It is also categorized by the inmates as a 'refugee camp', a 'prison camp', 'not a PoW [Prisoner of War] camp'. Interestingly, the iconic pictures of Fikret Alic- described here as 'pitifully thin' and

[9] It is again interesting to observe, in the context of the Campbell (2002a, 2002b) discussion initiated in chapter two, how the terms 'concentration camp' and 'extermination camp' seem to be interchangeable, and how the journalist, called to investigate allegations about the Serbs running 'concentration camps' readily confuses one of the characteristics technically associated with 'extermination camps'.

saying that Trnopolje has better conditions than his previous camp - that hit the world's television screens were taken at what appears to be the 'best' of the two camps. While the 'concentration camp' references make up the bulk of this article's Holocaust analogies there are two qualified references to 'genocide', made by the Bosnian Serbs, and one to the 'Nazi Holocaust', made by the reporter in a context of exasperated confusion over the various claims and counter-claims in this war.

The *Daily Mail*'s reporter, however, had no such ideational dilemmas on his page one story about the Bosnian camps. Suggestively entitled 'The Proof; Behind the barbed wire, the brutal truth about the suffering in Bosnia'[10], the Mail's article, based on the viewing of the famous television images, offers a degree of certainty, of "truth modality" (Fowler, 1991: 85), that Ed Vulliamy, who was actually there, did not dare to express in his story. Starting with a description of the terrible condition of the internees of Trnopolje – who are characterized as 'emaciated' and with 'sunken eyes' full of 'bewilderment' and 'beseeching inquiry' - the writer quickly instructs the reader on how to interpret these pictures: "They are the sort of scenes which flicker in black and white images from 50-year-old films of Nazi concentration camps" (Daily Mail, 1992a: n.p). While this is the only reference to 'Nazi concentration camps' in the entire article it is expressed in the language of a "straightforward truth claim" (Fowler, 1991: 86), excluding any other readings the viewer might make of these images. It also obscures where the term 'concentration camp' originated in relation to the Serbian camps – i.e. from the Bosnian government, as stated by Ed Vulliamy - effectively translating an official point of view into popular language (Fairclough, 1995) and presenting it as a certainty.

From then on, the article becomes neatly divided into what Van Dijk (1998) might call a classical polar structure of 'Perpetrator versus Victim', with the Bosnian Serbs filling the former category and the Bosnian Muslims occupying the latter. Thus the Serbs have set up 'brutal camps' to incarcerate 'their hated Moslem enemies'; they are 'well-fed', 'plump' and 'well-built', while complaining that there is a shortage of food to feed their prisoners; the Serbs run Omarska as if some 'madness' took over it; and their leader, Radovan Karadzic, is described by Channel Four's journalists as

[10] Included as Appendix 2

having no control over what is happening. The Muslims, on the other hand, with the 'haunted eyes', 'stubbled lantern jaws' and 'close-cropped heads' are described as 'lucky', because they are still standing - an indication of what might happen to them at any moment and another revealing indicator of the camp's true purpose. Any information that might "complicate any simple interpretation" (Vulliamy, 1992: n.p), to use an expression from the former article, is absent: there are no hints of claims and counter-claims regarding the camps, of Serbian refugees, or of young Muslims forced to fight: in short, there is nothing indicative of what Vulliamy called "the black absurdity of civil war" (Vulliamy, 1992a: n.p).

In this respect, the use of the Holocaust analogy has successfully accomplished a stereotyped presentation of the conflict. The sources in the *Mail's* article are either the journalists who visited the camps, or those sources indirectly presented through them. And the only time a Serbian source – Karadzic – is mentioned he is immediately disqualified by *Channel Four's* journalists as powerless, meaning that Karadzic's promise to punish the guilty is effectively rendered mute. A further look at both newspapers reveals some interesting information, even without the semiotic benefits of the original layout.

In *The Guardian's* case, the shadow of the Holocaust continues to hang very much on the rest of the edition. Following Vulliamy's page one article is Michael Simmons' report that "Iran vows to help end 'genocide'"[11] in Bosnia. Though the word 'genocide' appears in between quotation marks in the title and is later attributed in the story to the Iranian president, we learn that he is not the only world leader to think of Bosnia in those terms: "The Pope has joined in the arguments about concentration camps in Serbian-held areas" with the Vatican agreeing that there were "parallels between Nazism and human rights abuses in Bosnia" (Simmons, 1992: n.p). In this sense, the case for the use of the Holocaust analogy as a way to understand what is happening in Bosnia gains some momentum here. On the one hand, there is the leader of an important Islamic country decrying what is taking place in Bosnia as 'genocide' – a word associated, but by no means, exclusive to the events that took place in Nazi Germany - but on the other, there is the head of Christianity admitting that there *are*

[11] Included as Appendix 3

concentration camps in Bosnia comparable to the Nazi's. In short, the reader is left with a remarkably powerful inter-religious consensus on this subject that seems to further 'Holocaustize' its description.

Other articles in this edition of *The Guardian* detail a horrific torture performed by a laughing, 18 year old, Serbian woman at a concentration camp in Brcko. It is notable for two reasons: firstly, because the term concentration camp is taken up in the reporter's voice for the first time; and secondly, because it contains a witnesses' reference to a Serbian dug 'mass grave'. The penultimate 'Reports' article refers to the possibility of Western intervention in the conflict in response to what president Bush Sr. called the 'genocidal process' in Bosnia, while revealing that the United States already knew about the existence of 'death camps' and 'concentration camps' inside the country – two references which are clearly attributed to a US embassy report. The final article reports on the response of Radovan Karadzic, promising international access to the camps. The *Daily Mail* includes two more 'Reports' articles referring, respectively, to John Major's reluctance to use air strikes, for fear of killing innocent bystanders, and president Bush's insistence on the use of air power. Of the 'Editorial' pieces present in both newspapers, there is one worth mentioning, if only for its famous byline: 'Why the West must Act' by former British prime-minister Margaret Thatcher. It is notable for being a prime example of how the Holocaust can be used as a call to arms (Desch, 2006). Taking the side of the 'victims and losers', Lady Thatcher's opinion piece clearly describes the Bosnian war as an aggression planned and perpetrated by the Bosnian Serbs – whose 'ethnic cleansing strategy' is described as a combination of 'the barbarities of Hitler's and Stalin's policies' – with coordination and logistical support from Belgrade. Thus the West should intervene to stop the Serbian aggression and stop the war before it spills over with refugees, terrorist attacks, or a larger Balkan war. In short, the war should be controlled and stopped before it seriously threatens Western interests (Thatcher, 1992).

To say these first editions analyses offer a template for the remainder of the week is not entirely inappropriate, but requires further clarification. Regarding the use of the Holocaust analogy, it continues to appear in most of the *Mail's* articles in much the same way as in the above example: that is to say, the references are presented in the language of a 'truth claim' that frequently obscures its origins. Another consequence is that the Serbs continue to be very much the villains, and the Muslims their respective victims. As an example, the *Daily Mail's* readers had to wait four days to discover that *all* sides ran detention camps, while *Guardian* readers discovered it the following day.

However, when the *Mail* reported, on August 14th, that the International Red Cross had found conditions in every side's camps to be appalling, and demanded their instant closure for violating human rights and the Geneva Convention, the reporter immediately followed that revelation with a demand by Paddy Ashdown, the then Liberal Democrat Leader, to the Red Cross insisting on finding out what they intended to do in order "to curb the Serbs' 'Nazi-style' excesses" (Daily Mail, 1992b: n.p). That the term 'Nazi-style' appears to come from the reporter and not from the politician only underscores who the journalist considers to be the true villains of this piece – even in an article that was supposedly detailing the abuses perpetrated by all sides. And in case the reader still didn't get the point he learns, in the article's last paragraph, that a Serbian sniper just killed an American TV producer.

In this sense, and perhaps as expected, *The Guardian*'s coverage is remarkably different from the *Mail's* and, mirroring Vulliamy's article, considerably more cautious. That is to say, while it is not uncommon to find Holocaust analogies in *The Guardian's* articles they are usually not made in the reporter's voice, and are clearly attributed to a third party. The newspaper also seems to be significantly more preoccupied in avoiding a morally simplified presentation of the conflict. Thus when *The Guardian* first mentions the Red Cross findings, the newspaper stresses that even though all sides run atrocious detention camps the international media has focused almost exclusively on the Serbs'. And when it finally covers the release of the Red Cross report, it quotes the international body in accusing all groups of 'systematic brutality' in their respective detention camps and 'ethnic cleansing' strategies. Another article deconstructs any stereotyping even further by presenting a mortar attack on a UN compound in Sarajevo that might have been conducted by the Bosnian Muslims, which largely contradicts their 'pure' victim status. *The Guardian's* Bosnian war is, in this respect, noticeably more complex than the morally simplified version presented by the *Daily Mail*. The liberal newspaper was also the first to directly address the 'Holocaustization' of the conflict by publishing an article - entitled 'Nazi camps comparison is rejected' - where the reporter asks veteran Nazi-hunter Simon Wiesenthal to comment on the situation in Bosnia - who, as the title makes clear, disavows the comparison.

Interestingly, the majority of both newspapers' editorials are in accord, not only in diffusing the sensationalism created by ITN's pictures and its accompanying coverage but, also, in opposing the case for military intervention, and in particular, for British intervention. In this sense, they seem to clearly recognize how the 'Holocaustization' of the conflict carries with it an interventionist ideology that both newspapers, despite their traditional ideological differences, seem to explicitly reject.

3.2 August 13th-20th: The 'Butcher of Bosnia'

When General Radko Mladic, also known as the 'Butcher of Bosnia', overran the UN safe area of Srebrenica on July 12 1995 he not only humiliated the West by completely disregarding the concept of the safe areas, but he also created an humanitarian crisis the likes of which the world had not seen since the 1992 detention camps were exposed by the international media. Once again, the world's television screens were flooded with images of thousands of deportees, of women and children crying, of disturbing accounts of mass rape, and of reports detailing the chilling disappearance of thousands of Muslim boys and men taken by the Serb forces to be 'screened' as war criminals in what was to become known as Europe's first genocidal act since the end of the Second World War.

Table 3

July 13th – 20th	Reports	Editorials	**Total**
The Guardian	**29**	**10**	**39**
The Daily Mail	**10**	**2**	**12**
Total	**39**	**12**	**51**

Headlining its story 'Butcher moves in for the kill'[12], the *Daily Mail* once again quickly instructs its readers on how to make sense of the events it is about to describe.

[12] Included as Appendix 4

Thus on the story's third paragraph, the journalist informs the reader, once more in the language of a "straightforward truth claim" (Fowler, 1991: 86), that what is happening in Srebrenica has 'chilling echoes of the Nazi Holocaust'. From then on, the *Mail*'s description of the fall of Srebrenica is effectively 'Holocaustized', and its significance in the context of the Bosnian conflict gains the now familiar contours of this practice. A polar structure of 'Perpetrator versus Victim' (Van Dijk, 1998) is again present in the article, with the journalist's choice of vocabulary clearly dividing the Serb villains from the Muslim victims. In this sense, the lexical items chosen create tight categories: thus the Serbs have an 'iron grip' and carry with them the 'shadow of death'; they have 'terrifying' plans that cause 'horrible scene[s] of screaming' and 'panicking', of 'fright' and 'despair'; and their leader, Mladic, is the 'Butcher of Bosnia', a 'sinister shape'. Their victims are 'wretched hordes of helpless men, women and children ripe for ethnic cleansing'; 'very tired' and 'lacking everything'; enduring 'terrible' conditions, they are 'terrified', 'frightened', 'confused' and about to embark on a 'journey to genocide'.

Why the Serbs have conquered Srebrenica is never explained beyond the sum of their despicable actions. In fact, in the *Mail's* simplified account, their actions *are* the reason Srebrenica was taken. That is to say, the Serbs have taken the UN enclave because they are ruthless conquerors intent on ethnically cleansing the Bosnian Muslims, in raping 'thousands' of women and creating 'thousands' of refugees. Thus when both Mladic and Radovan Karadzic are quoted by the *Mail's* reporter describing Srebrenica as a 'terrorist stronghold' with 'small groups trying to put up resistance', their statements are immediately disqualified by the surrounding paragraphs, that only speak about their innocent victims. In this sense, one cannot help but recall Fairclough's statement that "equity and balance cannot be assessed by merely noting which voices are represented, and [...] how much space is given to each" (Fairclough, 1995: 81).

Thus, when Mladic speaks about separating the men to screen them for 'possible war criminals' (already in quotation marks in the original newspaper report), the reader knows that this is just a hypocritical excuse for the massacre that was about to take place. Only near the end of the story does the reader discover that Mladic might also have been searching for the 'Moslem guerrilla chieftain Nasir Oric' who has 'killed scores of Serbs in east Bosnia over the last three years' and disappeared into the 'hills overlooking Srebrenica' before the takeover. In this sense, it is briefly suggested that

Srebrenica might have harboured more than just innocent victims. But to unravel the *Mail's* only small hint of moral complexity one has to go beyond our sample.

For example, one has to open the *Washington Post* of 16 February 1994 to discover that Nasir Oric is a 'Moslem guerrilla chieftain' who liked to entertain journalists with videotapes of burned "Serb houses and headless Serb men, their bodies crumpled in a pathetic heap" (Pomfret, 1994: n.p). That he showed these videotapes in the comfort of his Srebrenica home, with 24 hour electricity in a town where "most people spend their days and nights without electricity" (Pomfret 1994: n.p). That he was the biggest fuel dealer in Srebrenica, a war profiteer, occasionally using the safe area to "take potshots at the 3,500 well-armed Serbs besieging Srebrenica" (Pomfret, 1994: n.p).

In this sense, *The Guardian's* edition of July 13 is much more successful in presenting a complex picture of the fall of Srebrenica. Thus *The Guardian's* readers learn in one report that the Bosnian government was "refusing to acquiesce in the ethnic cleansing by receiving the refugees in its territory" (Traynor, 1995a: n.p), a position that might be considered morally dubious (the *Mail's* readers had to wait another day to discover this). In another news story, the reader also learns that there are poorly defended Bosnian Serb villages around Srebrenica, one of which was recently attacked by the Bosnian Muslims. That the conquest of Srebrenica actually *has* military objectives – "to neutralise the Muslim threat, free manpower and remove an obstacle to [the Serb's] longstanding aim to enjoy full control of eastern Bosnia" (Traynor, 1995b: n.p). Or that the UN issued a resolution condemning the Serb offensive and demanding "that they and the Bosnian government respect the 'safe area' in accordance with the April 1993 demilitarisation agreement, which neither side fully implemented" (Black, 1995: n.p). All in all, a very different picture from the 'Holocaustized' version presented by the *Daily Mail*, with its stereotyped presentation of the conflict, and the simplified language of a morality play (Moeller, 1998b).

Needless to say that the differences between the 'Holocaustized' stories of the *Daily Mail* and their more balanced equivalents in *The Guardian* continue to be striking over the following days. A story published in both newspapers about the harrowing suicide of a twenty-year old Muslim girl in a makeshift UN refugee camp in Tuzla provides another revealing example[13]. Starting its article with a description of how the girl committed suicide and speculating about the possible reasons – rape being the chief amongst them - the *Daily Mail* again tells the reader, towards the end of the story, how to interpret the plight of the camp's twenty thousand refugees: they are 'terrifyingly reminiscent of humanity's darkest hour – the Nazi Holocaust'. Comment from the UN comes only in the form of an aid worker who suggests to the *Mail's* reporter that it is more urgent to take care of the living, which leads the journalist to dramatically state, towards the report's conclusion, that the girl's fate might have been a lucky one, comparing to what probably awaits the other refugees, i.e. systematic, mass extermination at the hands of the 'Serb legions'.

While *The Guardian's* article[14] starts in much the same way - describing the girl's suicide and the terrible conditions at this makeshift refugee camp – the differences soon become evident. For a start, there is no 'Holocaustization' of the scene and as a consequence it becomes inevitably complexified. Such as when a UN official states that the Bosnian government not only failed to provide any help but *actually* hindered the relief efforts because it "saw a symbolic value in heaping them [the refugees] all on the UN's lap" (Borger, 1995: n.p). However, just because the reporter doesn't 'Holocaustize' the scene doesn't mean the Serb's atrocities are not effectively conveyed. Nor does he shy away from showing the reader how they should be read, painting the Bosnian Serbs as murderous racists by translating a song lyric – "Die you scum, the Serbs are the champions. Come out on to your balconies and hail the white Serb race" (Borger, 1995: n.p) - which the conquerors have been transmitting into the fallen enclave. But to find evidence of 'Holocaustization' in the liberal newspaper's pages one has to wait until French president Jacques Chirac compares the West's inaction to the Western appeasement of Hitler in the 1930's.

Outside of that, only an 'Editorial' piece by journalist Ed Vulliamy[15], who broke the detention camp story in 1992, directly 'Holocaustizes' the conflict for *The Guardian's* readers. Summoning a range of historical analogies that start with the Spanish civil war of 1936 the Serbs are, in the author's opinion, Europe's new fascists.

[13] Included as Appendix 5
[14] Included as Appendix 6
[15] Included as Appendix 7

This editorial is particularly interesting to analyze because it not only shows the simplifying effects of such comparisons but it also demonstrates how they serve as part of a "rethoric arsenal" (Mamdani, 2007: n.p) employed to aggressively fix the discursive boundaries on Bosnia. Thus we learn in the fifth paragraph of this 'Editorial' piece that "any attempt to simplify the war into a tragedy of aggression, resistance and betrayal is muddled by pedantry and disinformation, usually from UN sources" (Vulliamy, 1995: n.p), who have committed the crime of criticising the Bosnian government's actions. That is to say, morally complexifying the war has been a smokescreen for non-intervention: the war is actually a simple affair – and thus one where it *is* possible to intervene – and those who think otherwise are pedants and disinformers. Chief among them is the UN because it dares to present some of the Bosnian government's actions as morally dubious, as demonstrated in the previous articles analysed. Obviously, no proof is offered to back up this claim, but since this is an 'Editorial' piece, none is presumably needed. To better understand this animosity, one again has to use outside sources to discover that some in the UN thought the international media were

> very, very biased in favour of the Bosnian government [and] intractably critical of the United Nations [...] blamed [...] for not being tougher with the Bosnian Serbs, whom they deemed the unofficially convicted demons in the Bosnian drama (Corwin, 1999: 8).

Or that "the oversimplified view of the Bosnian civil war [presented] by the press actually undermined the peace process" (Corwin, 1999: 8).

Vulliamy continues by stating that those who thought that "the defeat of the Third Reich meant that the bullies of history need not triumph in Europe, [...] were wrong" (Vulliamy, 1995: n.p), as the Serb's freedom from punishment now demonstrates. But again, the line is drawn between those who believe in the atrocities, and those who "smudge the horrors with words" (Vulliamy, 1995: n.p). Again there is a certain amount of 'symbolic violence' directed at those who don't agree with the author's take on Bosnia: they distort what is happening, and since what is happening is similar to what happened in the Third Reich, those who deny it are, presumably, the Bosnian equivalents of a Holocaust denier. That is why they will not hear "criticism of Serbian pogroms in Bosnian, and refuses to call them such" (Vulliamy, 1995: n.p). For those misguided enough to value Serbia's alliance with the allied powers in the Second World War, Vulliamy reminds them that "the Serbian Nazi puppet regime and Chetnik support for Hitler are overlooked" (Vulliamy, 1995: n.p). An interesting proposition that might be similar to suggesting that France's role in the Second World War should be rethought principally around Vichy. When Vulliamy finally concedes that there were Muslim atrocities, he immediately reduces them to "a few isolated, wild, excursions out of Goradze and Srebrenica" (Vulliamy, 1995: n.p).

Again, this analysis's idea is not to contradict the demonstrated fact that the Serbs were the main culprits, but to highlight that such historical comparisons usually have an agenda – in this case outside military intervention – and that they minimize, omit or distort any facts that might complicate, and thus hinder the user's objective.

Chapter 4 - Analysis and Conclusions

Having presented the principal highlights from our two week analysis of *The Guardian* and the *Daily Mail*, it is now time to extract some conclusions. Namely, how does this analysis answer this dissertation's twin research questions: "To what extent was the journalistic coverage of the Bosnian war 'Holocaustized'?" and "What was the nature of this 'Holocaustization'?"

The first concerns the value of analysing the use of the Holocaust analogy in the context of the Bosnian conflict. Was it worth analysing the coverage from this perspective? Was it sufficiently 'Holocaustized' to merit its study? The answer is a resounding 'yes'. From the twenty-eight editions analysed, it is estimated that 61, 5 % of their content was 'Holocaustized', meaning, that more than half of the editions contained at least one reference to our Holocaust category. The second conclusion is that the 'Holocaustization' of the conflict presented itself differently in the two newspapers and in the two time periods. In this sense, the first thing that should be recalled is that the amount of coverage given to Bosnia by both newspapers was inversely proportional to their respective readerships. That is to say, while the six million strong readers of the *Daily Mail* were rarely treated to more than two articles per edition, the much less read *Guardian* offered its readers extensive news reports on Bosnia that could reach a maximum of eight such pieces per edition. The second important point to notice concerns the qualitative difference in their coverage: while *Guardian* articles ran the gamut of war-topics – from stories related to outside intervention to others detailing the lack of coffin wood in Sarajevo – the *Daily Mail* sticks mostly to the main events of the war. But having said that, it is important to add that approximately 86 % of the *Mail's* articles on Bosnia were either page one or page two articles, and thus very prominent.

The two time periods also reveal important differences. For instance, if the graveness of the events taking place in the summer of 1995 easily rivalled those in 1992, the total amount of coverage given to Srebrenica by *The Guardian* and the *Daily Mail* was significantly less: 51 articles, as opposed to the 75 written by both newspapers in the summer of 1992. While this analysis is not qualified to provide a reason for this diminution one can speculate that perhaps the British newspapers were also suffering from 'Bosnia fatigue', as happened in the Dutch press (Ruigrok, de Ridder & Scholten, 2005). But whatever the reason, it is important to point out that *The Guardian* spearheaded this reduced interest, publishing twenty less articles than in the above analysed week of August 1992 – as opposed to the *Daily Mail* who decreased its coverage by just three articles.

A third point to make concerns how the Holocaust analogy was presented in both newspapers. In *The Guardian's* case, the direct use of the Holocaust analogy was clearly not encouraged, and when it appeared it was usually attributed to a third party. That means that the liberal newspaper, in most cases, 'imported' this 'Holocaustization', effectively recognizing that there were actors in the Bosnian conflict pushing for its application, but rarely endorsing it directly. The *Daily Mail,* on the other hand, adopted it directly, and some of the Holocaust analogies found were made by the journalists, which effectively meant that the newspaper clearly endorsed it as an appropriate way to interpret the conflict. This makes for some interesting differences between both dailies, which can be further highlighted by going back to our analysis of the first articles of 1992.

For example, in Vulliamy's 'Shame of camp Omarska' article, the main implication of using the Holocaust analogy seemed to be the confusion it generated. In this sense, the reporter recalled Desch (2006) when he exasperatedly complained that the lack of transparency in this war had to be penetrated to "uncover the miasma of lies, propaganda, exaggeration, denial, comparisons with the Nazi Holocaust [and] claims and counter-claims about concentration camps" (Vulliamy, 1992: n.p). In this respect, the Holocaust analogy was not used here as a call for military intervention, nor was it taken up by the reporter as a way to call attention. There was also evidence of some effort by the journalist to contradict the possible stereotyping effects of this practice, by providing accounts of Serb refugees, and of Muslims who employ a 13 year old fighter: that is to say, none of the factions of the war looked particularly wholesome. The journalist's cautiousness also revealed another important thing: that 'Holocaustizing' had not yet fixed the boundaries of the journalistic discourse on Bosnia. This is especially striking when one considers that the same author had completely discarded this cautiousness three years later, in his 1995 historically charged 'Editorial'. But more importantly, it reveals another significant difference between both newspapers' coverage: the emphasis they place on objectivity. In this sense, *The Guardian* seems to demand a greater degree of balance and detachment from those reporters involved in covering the more factual 'Reports', as opposed to the *Daily Mail*, who seems to give them more leverage. This would partly explain Ed Vulliamy's cautiousness in writing his 'Report' about the 1992 Serbian detention camps as opposed to his charged 'Editorial' in 1995. The other part of this explanation might just be found in the fact that 'Holocaustizing' had firmly become entrenched as a discursive practice in 1995. On the other hand, three years is also a long time, and maybe the author genuinely changed his mind on how he felt about the conflict. Nevertheless, there is a point to be made in the fact that he expressed his changed opinion in the form of an 'Editorial'.

However, the main difference between both newspapers is not that the Holocaust analogy is less present in *The Guardian* than in the *Daily Mail*, but rather, that it is presented quite distinctly in both newspapers. Again, a different emphasis on objectivity seems to offer a convincing explanation for this. In *The Guardian's* pages, and especially in the week of August of 1992, the Holocaust analogy is, in most cases, clearly presented as one of the possible ways to interpret what was going on in Bosnia-Herzegovina, but it is rarely adopted by the journalists who are writing the articles, which shows the newspaper's reluctance to fully present the conflict in this particular light. This makes for a telling difference because the reporter – the one who is describing to the audience events that happened in the world beyond their personal experience (Fowler 1991) – does not directly tell them that that is the best way to read the events. But having said that, can one really argue that *The Guardian's* coverage is significantly less 'Holocaustized' than the *Daily Mail's*? In this sense, it is again important to recall Fairclough's (1995) statement that ideologies are made more effective by being rendered invisible. That is to say, that the articles that are indirectly 'Holocaustized' and the way they present, frame, legitimise or marginalise the different voices, are frequently conveying to their readers certain ideological positions – be they military intervention or humanitarian compassion – without necessarily revealing their discursive strategy. In this respect, one can legitimately argue that writing an article that places the Pope's endorsement of the Nazi concentration camp comparisons side by side with the Iranian president's claim of genocide in Bosnia - without any conflicting opinion in the middle - might be an effective way to convey the reporter's point without directly stating it.

In this sense, one can argue that while *The Guardian's* greater sense of objectivity always meant that the Holocaust analogy was presented as one of the possible ways to interpret the conflict, this might not amount to much, since it was always the dominant way to interpret the conflict, even if the journalists never adopted it directly. That is to say, the Holocaust analogy was always omnipresent in the liberal newspaper's coverage. Which signifies that while a greater sense of balance and detachment might have led *The Guardian* to always attribute the comparison to a third party, or to even bother to write an article where an expert directly disavowed this interpretive framework, the fact remains that it was still *the* main interpretive framework being offered to the audience. Meaning, that either the liberal newspaper directly presented the facts of the war without resorting to any comparison or, when a comparison was made, it was usually the Holocaust analogy, even if it was always attributed to outside sources. In this sense, there was no alternative discursive strategy to compete with the Holocaust analogy. Interestingly, and going back to the conclusion of this dissertation's theoretical chapter, journalistic practices such as objectivity might have actually contributed to the perpetuation of this particular discursive practice. Since the journalist's need to be balanced meant that the Holocaust analogy ended up always being reproduced – even when it was contradicted – the discursive boundaries of what could be said about the Bosnian conflict were continually revolving around the use of the Holocaust.

However, when the Holocaust analogy is directly adopted by the journalist who is writing the story, as happens mainly in the *Daily Mail*, its implications become more readily visible. For instance, those articles that are fully 'Holocaustized' present a simplified, depoliticised, version of events, usually in the language of a morality play - as suggested by many of the authors reviewed in this dissertation. That is to say, not only are the events presented powerfully simplified by this analogy, but they are also thoroughly decontextualized and offered "as part of an eternal encounter between evil and innocence" (Mamdani, 2007: n.p). This was evident from our analysis of the *Mail's* first article, entitled 'The Proof', where 'Holocaustizing' had clearly succeeded in simplifying the conflict: as Moeller (1999b) stated there was a group characterized as unequivocally evil (the Serbs) and another as *the* victims (the Bosnian Muslims) - with the reporter's job being to spread "the news of their plight to the rest of the world" (Daily Mail, 1992a: n.p). In this sense, the *Mail's* articles are less objective than the *Guardian's*: they don't have the liberal newspaper's sense of balance and detachment, which made their articles at least try to contradict the stereotypes and simplifications implicit in the Holocaust analogy.

The articles that are directly 'Holocaustized' also exhibit a certain amount of common characteristics. For a start, they usually have what Van Dijk (1998) would call a polar structure of 'Perpetrator versus Victim', which quickly tells the reader who is morally right to side with. This structure is constructed by the lexical items chosen to describe the protagonists of these stories: that is to say, the expressions chosen to describe them convey a wealth of ideological positions, typically by choosing terms that "express a value judgement" (Van Dijk, 1998: 31). Thus those who fall in the 'Perpetrator' category, in our case the Serbs, are described with terms that accentuate their barbarism, their despicable intentions, their overall negativity; the 'Victims', on the other hand, are usually described as 'frightened', 'confused', 'wretched', or in any other terms destined to highlight their innocence - their positivism, so to speak. These dual categories are, in this respect, water-tight: they do not mix, and the articles have to be written in a way that minimizes or eliminates any risk of contagion - which might confuse the reader on whom he is supposed to side with. This is done in several ways.

One of them is through the successful translation of official points of view into popular language (Fairclough, 1995), frequently obscuring their origin, such as when the *Daily Mail* employs the term 'concentration camp' without telling the readers that it came from the Bosnian government. Or when the *Mail* fails to mention that the Bosnian government was refusing to take in refugees from Srebrenica. Another is through what is called the text's 'unmentionables' (Van Dijk, 1998), namely, any elements that might complicate their simplified structure, usually information that would cast doubt on the victims' 'pure' status. That is to say, there is virtually no distinction between the victims and the war faction they belong to. Meaning, that if the Bosnian Muslims are the victims, then *all* of them are innocent, and there is no difference between the Muslim government, the Muslim fighters, and the Muslim refugees. On the other hand, there can also be no information on Serb victims, as presented by Vulliamy in his 1992 article for

The Guardian, since this would complicate this polar structure. Obviously, these 'unmentionables' contribute very much to Fairclough's (1995) 'translation of ideology idea', since it is not hard to imagine that this might have been the way the Muslim government wished the war was presented. But they are also a manifestation of what Desch (2006) complained about regarding the use of this analogy: namely, that it obfuscates the facts on the ground, prevents conflicts from being judged on their own merits, and obscures the limits of what can be done to solve them.

Another factor that reinforces this structural composition is the articles' high degree of "truth modality", where value statements are usually presented as a "straightforward truth claim" (Fowler, 1991: 85-86). This means that articles that are directly 'Holocaustized' are written in a more authoritative manner, no doubt intended to erase any hesitation the reader might entertain on how to interpret the events and which of the protagonists it is morally 'right' to side with. This means that these articles fix the discursive boundaries on Bosnia in a more aggressive way, since they carry with them at least one explicit ideology: that barbarism cannot be tolerated. And since barbarism is only associated with one of the main protagonists of the conflict, what can be said, and possibly thought, about Bosnia cannot contradict this main 'fact', unless the reader wants to be associated with those who encourage barbarism. This is well demonstrated in Vulliamy's 1995 editorial, where a certain amount of 'symbolic violence' is employed to aggressively define the boundaries of the discourse on Bosnia - what LaCapra called the "self-righteous use of the Holocaust as 'symbolic capital'" (cited in Friedlander 1992: 112). In this sense, the *Daily Mail's* 'Holocaustization' operates in a very different way than *The Guardian's*. That is to say, while both newspapers' coverage of the conflict is very much 'Holocaustized', they differ in one fundamental way: while the liberal newspaper is never able to offer an alternative to this discursive practice, and ends up presenting it as the dominant way to interpret the conflict, the *Mail* goes farther and presents it as the *unequivocal* way to make sense of what was happening in Bosnia-Herzegovina.

Why these differences? One can only speculate, but one of the reasons might have to do with the newspapers' distinct readerships and editorial positions. With six million readers, the *Daily Mail* might be more prone to the appeal of a powerful simplifying tool that made the Bosnian conflict instantly accessible to its readers. *The*

Guardian, on the other hand, has a significantly smaller target audience, made up of the higher crusts of society, and more open to a complex picture of events. Another reason certainly lies in the newspapers' different application of the ideal of objectivity, with the liberal newspaper exhibiting a higher degree of detachment and balance on its factual 'Reports' than the *Daily Mail*. .This also accounts for the *Mail's* considerably more 'charged' language, which usually employs value-laden lexical items, as opposed to the liberal newspaper's more cautious, and 'neutral' terms. But in the end, why was the Holocaust analogy so omnipresent in both newspapers' coverage? Why did it become the dominant discursive strategy to present the audience to the tragic events unfolding in Bosnia-Herzegovina? While this analysis cannot offer a definitive answer, a tentative one, can at least be offered at the end of this dissertation:

For the majority in the United Kingdom for whom Bosnia, Croatia, and Serbia were little more than unspecified parts of the former Yugoslavia, at best known for their holiday potential, there was the urgent need to provide them with a familiar and attractive doorway into a conflict that was simultaneously dramatic and undeniably intricate. Considering that journalists tend to focus on the human side of any conflict and that some of the horrors befalling the victims were historically resonant, it is not hard to understand how the Holocaust analogy was a convenient parallel to establish. In this sense, it helped solve many of the conundrums that usually plague the reporter's presentation of a complex foreign conflict. For a start, it succeeded in grabbing the audience's attention to a conflict that might otherwise have been ignored (Powers 1999). Secondly, it turned a complex war into a digestible one, always providing unfamiliar British audiences with a peg to hold on to one of the most morally duplicitous and Byzantine conflicts of recent European history. And lastly, it was a morally effective way to generate enough public outrage to appeal for outside military intervention, to try and stop the barbarisms taking place in Europe's most problematic backyard.

Afterword

"One's memory of [...] history, can be influenced by the news especially when the audience does not have relevant knowledge and experience of their own on which they can rely" - Findhal

Now that we have reached the end of this dissertation, it is time to reflect on what was achieved, what problems were encountered along the way, and which contribution, if any, did this dissertation provide to the larger field of news discourse analysis.

When the time came to write this dissertation I had one principal idea: to investigate the implications of what I considered to be a very powerful comparison – the Holocaust analogy – and the possible effects this practice might have on the object being compared, in this case, the 1992-1995 Bosnian conflict. There is no novelty in saying that analogies are, in their essence, simplifying procedures, and that journalism is, by its very nature, prone to use these devices as much as possible. Nevertheless, I still thought that comparing something to the Holocaust, frequently and rightly considered humanity's darkest hour, risks not just facilitating access to the compared object, but actually irrevocably *changing* it, especially if there are any doubts regarding the similarities. The problem was not that there weren't similarities between some of the things that happened in the Bosnian conflict and some of the horrors perpetrated by the Nazis during the Second World War. The question was: are these similarities profound enough to merit such an enormous comparison? Or is this comparison going to operate as a restrictive discursive practice, arguably limiting the complexity of the Bosnian conflict?

Equating an event to the Holocaust has serious implications. As Susan D. Moeller explains, comparing

> a crisis to the Holocaust is an exercise in moral equivalence; it signals to readers and viewers the scale of deaths in a crisis as well as the intent of the murderers (Moeller, 1999b: 5).

That is to say, if what was happening in Bosnia was similar to the Holocaust then the Bosnian Serbs and their sponsors were intent in the systematic, industrialized, mass extermination of every single Bosnian Muslim. They were not just the protagonists of a civil war anymore: they were *the* aggressors in a war motivated not so much by territorial conquest but by racial extermination. That means that if they ran 'Nazi style' concentration camps, their 'ethnic cleansing' strategy was not so much a despicable attempt to terrorize the Muslim population into vacating territory but part of an intention to mass exterminate them, like the Nazi's did with the Jews. And if journalists were signalling to their audiences that this was what was happening in Bosnia, no morally responsible person should stand idly by and allow this to happen. On the other hand, there were legitimate doubts about the appropriateness of this discursive practice as an adequate way to introduce unfamiliar audiences to the dramatic events unfolding in Bosnia - which led me to investigate what implications it might have.

Since the word 'implication' opens the door to a multiplicity of investigative avenues my first problem was to choose just what 'implications' would I analyse in the context of this dissertation. Despite the multiple roads I might have chosen, I decided to focus on empirically ascertaining the extent to which there was evidence of 'Holocaustization' in the Bosnian war and discussing the nature of this discursive practice. In this sense, I wanted very much to investigate just *what* happens to an article that is 'Holocaustized'. How is information conveyed? Is there any underlying ideology to 'Holocaustized' articles, and how does it manifest itself? How does this comparison condition the interpretation of the events being described in the article? And what are the processes through which this occurs? At the same time, I was also aware that this discursive practice might have limiting effects for the journalistic discourse on the Bosnian war as a whole, and I was very much interested in discussing this.

Considering the limitations of my empirical analysis, I have to conclude that I was much more successful in demonstrating in what ways the Holocaust analogy conditioned the journalistic articles in which it appears, than in demonstrating the long term effects it might have had on the journalistic discourse on Bosnia. In this sense, I think that my very modest contribution to the field of news discourse analysis comes in the form of highlighting the common characteristics of these 'Holocaustized' articles.

And even in this area, I have to restrict my success more to the articles that were directly 'Holocaustized' by the journalists as opposed to those where the Holocaust analogy was present, but not adopted in the voice of the reporter. Concerning the former, I consider that I was able to extract a number of common characteristics that might be helpful in the analysis of other articles of conflicts that have or will be 'Holocaustized'. In this respect, I dare say there will be many similarities: in structure, modality, lexical items employed and the texts' 'unmentionables', to name just a few. Obviously, I am very much indebted to the technical and theoretical expertise of the many authors discussed in this dissertation, who provided me with the tools necessary to arrive at these conclusions.

Regarding the articles where the Holocaust analogy is attributed to a third party, I feel a longer and more longitudinal analysis would be required before extracting any relevant conclusions. In my short study, I saw diversity rather than a common pattern - as opposed to the articles where the analogy was taken up in the reporter's voice. For instance, in some cases, like in Ed Vulliamy's 1992 article, the writer would show and transmit uncertainty towards its use; other articles would generate such a powerful consensus, such as when both the Pope and the president of Iran agreed on it, that the journalist's direct endorsement was barely needed; yet in others, such as the articles relating to Chirac's 'appeasement' tirade, the journalists would actively disqualify the comparison as exaggerated or frame it as a political strategy, effectively disavowing it. However, it is not known if a sustained analysis would have revealed a more persistent pattern in these cases. But one thing is certain: its indirect use did not change the fact that it still was *the* dominant discursive strategy being presented to the audience to make sense of what was happening in Bosnia-Herzegovina.

I also think this dissertation was successful in demonstrating, through the analysis of these processes and the theoretical discussion it promoted, how the media tackle complex foreign conflicts and what can be the consequences of the discursive strategies they choose to present unfamiliar situations to their home audiences. However, this particular discursive practice arguably presented a very restricted interpretation of what was happening in Bosnia-Herzegovina. In this sense, I feel this dissertation managed to demonstrate how 'Holocaustizing', at its best, generated confusion on how to interpret some of the events unfolding and how, at its worse, it actually simplified those events, arguably changing them by withholding information, distorting them, or minimizing their importance – a situation which is especially evident in the side by side comparison of 1995's 'Holocaustized' *Daily Mail* articles and their *Guardian* counterparts.

It also shows how this particular analogy carries with it a wealth of ideological positions, chief among them outside military intervention. In this respect, I feel that the reader is actually one of the main losers of this discursive practice, since his admission ticket to the Bosnian conflict came at the cost of being denied the chance to view a substantial part of the picture. Furthermore, his seat was mostly subordinated to the journalist's or a third party's agenda. But I am also convinced that this practice had important limiting effects on the whole of the journalistic discourse on Bosnia, though I was not able to prove this through my analysis, merely to hint at it in my theoretical discussion. In order to prove any limiting effects, a much more exhaustive analysis would have had to have been conducted, one that would've focused, for instance, on comparing the various British newspapers to ascertain if which alternative interpretations were decisively left out of the media's coverage.

But in the end, what is the true relevance of this dissertation to the wider field of media studies? After all, isn't it widely known that journalism is the art of the cliché? So what makes the Holocaust analogy so important to merit such a detailed analysis? In my opinion, the relevance of analysing the Holocaust analogy – and other similarly powerful discursive strategies – derives from the fact that they are extreme cases of what is part and parcel of the journalistic profession: symbolism, stereotypes, comparisons and rhetorical shortcuts. That is to say, they belong to that category of discursive practices that, while seeking to facilitate an object's comprehension, actually end up *changing* the reported object. Thus instead of simplifying the Bosnian conflict 'Holocaustizing' actually *became* part of the conflict. Suddenly, reporting events had to be subordinated to checking the validity of this interpretative matrix, with some thinking that a new Holocaust was taking place in Bosnia and passionately encouraging outside intervention, and others cautioning against it. What was truly happening in Bosnia seemed sometimes to be overshadowed by what *might* be happening in Bosnia - to the arguable detriment of us all.

It thus becomes vitally important that the consequences of these discursive practices be thoroughly discussed amongst the members of the journalistic profession and in the halls of academia. If not, some of the repercussions of this type of journalism might start to look increasingly like the results of this study, conducted in the Swedish town of Umea:

> A massacre committed by Croatian armed forces in the autumn of 1993 in Bosnia was front-page news for a couple of days in Swedish newspapers. One year later, most people still remembered the vivid pictures of the massacre. However, their interpretation of the pictures changed. Where they said in 1993 that the Croatian forces committed the atrocities, one year later the Serbs replaced the Croats and the Croatian massacre had become a Serb massacre. The pictures remained the same, the context changed according to a general picture about the Bosnian war that was presented in the international media. The Serbs were the bad guys, the Muslims the victims (Findahl cited in Ruigrok, de Ridder, Scholten, 2005: 179).

And history was effectively re-written in the audience's mind.

***

Bibliography

Bell, Martin (1998) 'The Journalism of attachment' in Kieran, Matthew (ed.) *Media Ethics*, London, Routledge.

Borger, Julian (1995) 'Lonely death in a crowded cornfield', *The Guardian*, 15 July 1995: 12.

Bourdieu, Pierre (1991) *Language and Symbolic Power*, Cambridge, Polity Press.

Bourdieu, Pierre (1998) *On Television and Journalism*, London, Pluto Press.

Bourdieu, Pierre (1989) 'Social Space and Symbolic Power', *Sociological Theory* 7, 1: 14-25.

Bourdieu, Pierre (1983) 'The Forms of Capital' at http://www.viet-studies.org/Bourdieu_capital.htm (Accessed: 7 March 2007)

Boyd, Charles G. (1995) 'Making Peace with the Guilty: The Truth about Bosnia', *Foreign Policy* 74, 5: 22-38

Burns, John (1996) 'The Media as Impartial Observers or Protagonists: Conflict Reporting or Conflict Encouragement in Former Yugoslavia' in Gow, James, Paterson, Richard & Preston, Alison (Eds.) *Bosnia by television*, London, British Film Institute.

Campbell, David (2002a) 'Atrocity, memory, photography: imaging the concentration camps of Bosnia – the case of ITN versus Living Marxism, Part 1', *Journal Of Human Rights* 1, 1: 1–33.

Campbell, David (2002b) 'Atrocity, memory, photography: imaging the concentration camps of Bosnia – the case of ITN versus Living Marxism, Part 2', *Journal Of Human Rights* 1, 2: 143–172.

Corwin, Phillip (1999) *Dubious Mandate. A Memoir of the UN in Bosnia, Summer 1995*, Durham, Duke University Press.

Daily Mail (1992a) 'The Proof; Behind the barbed wire, the brutal truth about the suffering in Bosnia', *Daily Mail*, 7 August 1992: 1-2.

Daily Mail (1992b) 'Red Cross Horror at Bosnian Hell Camps', *Daily Mail*, 14 August 1992: 2.

Deacon, David, Pickering, Michael, Golding, Peter & Murdock, Graham (1998), *Researching Communications: A practical guide to methods in media and cultural analysis,* London, Arnold.

Desch, Michael C. (2006) 'The Myth of Abandonment: The Use and Abuse of the Holocaust Analogy', *Security Studies* 15, 1: 106-145.

Fairclough, Norman (1995) *Media Discourse*, London, Arnold.

Fowler, Roger (1991) *Language in the news: Discourse and ideology in the press,* London, Routledge.

Glenny, Misha (1996) *The Fall of Yugoslavia*, London, Penguin Books.

Hall, Stuart (Ed.) (1997) *Representation: Cultural Representations and Signifying Practices*, London, Sage.

Hammond, Philip & Herman, Edward S. (2000) *Degraded capability: the media and the Kosovo crisis*, London, Pluto Press.

Human Rights Watch (2006) *Weighing the Evidence: Lessons from the Slobodan Milosevic Trial* at http://hrw.org/reports/2006/milosevic1206/milosevic1206webwcover.pdf (Accessed 24 April 2007).

Knightley, Philip (2003) *The First Casualty: The War correspondent as hero, propagandist and myth-maker from the Crimea to Iraq*, London, Andre Deutsch.

LaCapra, Dominick (1992) 'Representing the Holocaust: Reflections on the Historian's Debate' in Fridlander, Saul, *Probing the limits of representation: Nazism and the "Final Solution"*, Cambridge, Massachusetts, Harvard University Press.

MacDonald, David Bruce (2002) *Balkan Holocausts? Serbian and Croatian victim-centred propaganda and the war in Yugoslavia*, Manchester, Manchester University Press.

Mamdani, Mahmood (2007) 'The Politics of Naming: Genocide, Civil War, Insurgency' in *London Review of Books* 29, 5 at http://www.lrb.co.uk/v29/n05/mamd01_.html (Accessed: 3 April 2007).

McLaughlin, Greg (2002) *The War Correspondent*, London, Pluto Press.

Moeller, Susan D. (1999a) *Compassion fatigue: How the media sell disease, famine, war, and death*, Great Britain, Routledge.

Moeller, Susan D. (1999b) 'Four Habits of International News Reporting' at http://www.frameworksinstitute.org/products/fourhabits.pdf (Accessed: 7 March 2007).

Pickering, Michael (2001) *Stereotyping: The Politics of Representation*, Houndmills, Palgrave.

Pomfret, John (1994) 'Weapons, Cash and Chaos Lend Clout to Srebrenica's Tough Guy', *Washington Post*, 16 February 1994: A14.

Postman, Neil (1985) *Amusing ourselves to death*. Middlesex, England, Penguin Books.

Power, Samantha (1999) 'To suffer by comparison?', *Daedalus* 128,2: 31-66.

Ruigrok, Nel, de Ridder, Jan. A., Scholten, Otto (2005) 'News Coverage of the Bosnian War in Dutch Newspapers: Impact and Implications' in Philip Seib (Ed.) *Media and conflict in the twenty-first century*, New York, Palgrave Macmillan.

Said, Edward (1997) *Covering Islam: How the media and the experts determine how we see the rest of the world,* London, Vintage Books.

Schrøder, Kim Christian (2002) 'Discourses of fact', in Jensen, Klaus Bruhn. (Ed.) *A Handbook of Media and Communication Research: Qualitative and quantitative methodologies*, London, Routledge. .

Simmons, Michael (1992) 'Iran vow to help end "genocide"', *The Guardian*, 7 August 1992: 6.

Simons, Marlise (2007), 'Serbs failed to stop genocide', *International Herald Tribune*, 26 February: 1.

Swastika. Reference.com. Crystal Reference Encyclopedia. Crystal Reference Systems Limited at http://www.reference.com/browse/crystal/30815 (Accessed: April 25, 2007).

Thatcher, Margaret (1992) 'We must act now before it's too late', *The Guardian*, 7 August 1992: 19.

Traynor, Ian (1995a) 'Serbs bus refugees to front line; Horror of ethnic cleansing returns', *The Guardian, 13* July 1995: 1.

Traynor, Ian (1995b) 'Third time unlucky for unsafe area', *The Guardian*, 13 July 1995: 11.

Van Dijk, Teun A. (1998) 'Opinions and Ideologies in the Press', in Bell, Allan & Garett, Peter (Eds.) *Approaches to Media Discourse*, Oxford, Blackwell Publishers.

Vulliamy, Edward (1992) 'Shame of Camp Omarska', *The Guardian,* 7 August 1992: 1.

Vulliamy, Edward (1995) 'For whom does the bell toll now?', *The Guardian*, 15 July 1995: 23.

Wieten, Jan (2002) 'Background and influence of media reporting of the conflict in the former Yugoslavia during the period 1991-1995: A study of views and methods of Dutch journalists' in NIOD (Netherlands Institute for War Documentation) *Srebrenica: Reconstruction, background, consequences and analyses of the fall of a safe area* at http://193.173.80.81/srebrenica/ (Accessed: 30 May 2007).

Appendices

Appendix 1 – 'Shame of Camp Omarska'

The Guardian (London)
August 7, 1992

SECTION: THE GUARDIAN HOME PAGE; Pg. 1

LENGTH: 2591 words

HEADLINE: SHAME OF CAMP OMARSKA;

We will not rest until the international community has gained access to all detention camps in Bosnia, President Bush said last night. Ed Vulliamy has already been inside several, including Omarska in north-eastern Serb-occupied Bosnia. Here, he provides the first eyewitness account in a British newspaper of the starvation and human rights abuses being inflicted on the captives

BYLINE: ED VULLIAMY

BODY:

"I DON'T want to tell any lies, but I cannot tell the truth," says the young man, emaciated, sunken-eyed, and attacking his watery bean stew like a famished dog, his spindly hands shaking.

This is lunchtime in the Omarska camp or "investigation centre" operated by the Bosnian-Serbian police for Muslim captives, near Prijedor in north-eastern Bosnia.

The internees are horribly thin, raw-boned; some are almost cadaverous, with skin like parchment folded around their arms; their faces are lantern-jawed, and their eyes are haunted by the empty stare of the prisoner who does not know what will happen to him next.

The prisoners, or internees, emerge from a huge rust-coloured shed, 30 at a time, into the sun and heat.

They are lined up by a prison guard, a civilian policeman, and then, as part of some pathetic camp drill, they run in single file across a courtyard and into the camp canteen, under the watchful eye of a beefy policeman with a machine gun in a glass observation post. There are no barked orders; they know the drill only too well.

In the well-kept kitchen they line up again and wait for their ration: a bowl of beans augmented with breadcrumbs and a piece of bread, which they wolf down in silence at the metal tables, before quickly and obediently forming another line by the door, and then running in line back across the yard, into the aluminium shed.

The meal takes five minutes. It appears to be their only one of the day. If they ate even twice as much they would be only slightly less gaunt and withered. Some take their bread with them to eat later. Then the next 30 appear, and jog across the yard.

Omarska is an old iron mine and ore processing plant. It is now the most notorious on a list published by the Bosnian government naming 57 of what it calls "concentration camps".

Neither the International Red Cross nor the United Nations - nor any press - had visited it before we arrived on Wednesday, although the international agencies have expressed acute concern about the Bosnian-Muslim allegations.

The unexpected and unexplained access to Omarska was part of an invitation by the Bosnian-Serbian president, Radovan Karazdic, a challenge to the Guardian and Independent Television News to inspect "whatever you wish to see" in response to the concentration camp allegations.

"I'll eat my lunch first, then talk," says Sebakoudin Elezovic. "Every day is the same, like this, just doing nothing and waiting to eat. The old people and children move on, I don't know where. "I was in the defence force - but not caught in a fight. I tried to get to Trnopolje transit camp [a civilian camp] but the army caught me on the way and brought me here."

Sebakoudin, who shows no signs of beating, says: "We are being investigated.

Because I know that nothing can be hidden, I tell the truth and hope I will be OK. If I am guilty, then I'll have to face the consequences. I speak only of myself - personally, nobody touched me."

And with that, unwilling to discuss the matter any further as the soldiers approach the table, he rises to make way for the next lunch shift.

Most of the inmates are too visibly terrified to talk. We decline to interview people selected by the authorities, preferring to try finding our own inmates to talk to, but we are bundled away upstairs for a briefing.

Omarska, they tell us, is an "investigation centre" for men suspected of being in the Muslim irregular army. They are rounded up or arrested, then "screened" to determine whether they are fighters or civilians.

Apart from their under nourishment and the humiliation of the drill, none of the 80 inmates we saw showed signs of violence or beating.

Those found to have "prepared the rebellion" go into "category A", explains the police chief's spokeswoman, Nada Balban. There have been 126. They are awaiting trial.

Those found to be fighters are "category B" and go eventually to a prisoner of war camp at Manjaca, to which the Red Cross has been admitted (and to which the Serbian military were eager to steer us, rather than Omarska), and then to a military court. There have been 1,290. Others go to the Trnopolje camp down the road, about which refugees have made some serious allegations - this is the biggest group, 1,400 strong.

Interestingly, Omarska and Trnopolje are run by the civil authorities, not the army.

Ms Balban admits: "No one is proud. There is shame here. If there is a place similar to this in Sarajevo, for our people, then let's change it . . . Yes, hostages of course, we do have some hostages for exchange. We have offered people since the first day of the war. But the other side does not want it."

Though this may be true of Omarska, it is generally untrue, since a camp we visited on the outskirts of Sarajevo has been established solely for the purpose of swapping Muslim captives for Serbs.

After the briefing, Dr Karazdic's invitation to us collapses. We ask to be shown into the rust-coloured shed and to see the sleeping quarters, workshops or whatever.

There is shooting in the woods near the camp (either a Muslim attack or a Serbian prank, it is impossible to tell), as there was around us as we arrived, and our safety is at risk, say the police.

Suggestions that we are safer in the camp than outside it are overruled.

Then Ms Balban explains: "The politicians are sitting on two chairs. They have their promises, but we have our procedures, and we cannot do everything.

You must know we have orders. You have your reasons, we have others. He [Dr Karazdic] promised us something else."

So the aluminium shed conceals some secret. It is a secret the international agencies must uncover if the miasma of lies, propaganda, exaggeration, denial, comparisons with the Nazi Holocaust, claims and counter-claims about concentration camps, is to be more than partially penetrated.

The International Red Cross and the UN have not been admitted, Ms Balban says, "because this is not a camp, it is a centre."

She claims that "there is no demand from them or anyone else to come here."

But, under pressure, she then promises: "We would allow them to come here Why not?"

Back in the town of Prijedor, women line the pavement outside police headquarters, waiting for transit papers to leave the area. Some say their menfolk had been in Omarska for four months.

Some of the inmates we were allowed to see had clearly not eaten properly for weeks or months. And although there was no visible evidence of serious violence, let alone systematic extermination, inside the aluminium shed is something it was worth them breaking Dr Karazdic's promise to avoid exposing.

Omarska has been visited by the Serbian-run Yugoslav Red Cross, and given a clean bill of health. Dr Dusko Ivic, working at the Trnopolje camp, said on Wednesday: "I have visited Omarska and my professional assessment about the health of the people is very good, apart from some diarrhoea."

Trnopolje camp, down another 10 miles of dirt road, is claimed by the Muslim government to be the second biggest "concentration camp". Here, Muslim doctors among the internees said people arrived from Omarska and another "investigation centre" at Kereter in terrible condition. Evidence was passed to the Guardian and ITN in the form of a roll of undeveloped film.

Here is complete confusion - political and physical. The camp is a ramshackle fenced-in compound around a former school. The men stand stripped to the waist, in their thousands, against the wire in the relentless afternoon heat; the women and children seek shade upstairs in the crowded, smelly building. They wait, stare at nothing, sweat - and wonder what will happen next.

One group has arrived from Kereter that morning, claiming that they had been beaten, but showing no signs of it. However, says pitifully thin Fikrit Alic: "It is worse than here. There is no food." Others in the group looked better fed. Another boy, Icic Budo, says "they killed 200 people" at Kereter and "many more at Omarska". He has seen no bodies himself, but another boy had seen one corpse near the main gate.

Trnopolje cannot be called a "concentration camp" and is nowhere as sinister as Omarska: it is very grim, something between a civilian prison and transit camp. The Yugoslav Red Cross has a small station here, and there are meagre cooking facilities.

These boys had been rounded up in their villages. Some call Trnopolje a refugee camp, but Fikrit Acic says: "It is a prison camp, but not a PoW camp. We are not fighters. They came to our village, Kozarac. [Now literally flattened byfighting.] I was near my house; they put us on the buses and brought us to Kereter for a while, and then here." Icic Budo adds: "The fact is, they do not want us to live here any more. They want us and our families to go, if we can find our families. I don't know where mine is."

But some people have fled voluntarily to Trnopolje simply to avoid the raging battles in the villages around. Inar Gornic, clutching her crying baby in what was the school "Foto Klub" room, says: "I came alone, from the Trnopolje village.

The conditions are very hard here, but there was terrible fighting and we had no food at all. It is safer here, but we don't know what kind of status we have.

We are refugees, but there are guards and the wire fence."

"No violence against us, just hot and smelly," adds her husband, vacantly, among the sea of rugs, sweaty blankets and the odd mattress strewn along the floors and corridors, while primative bread ovens are set up outside.

Stories in Trnopolje, more freely told than at Omarska, are brimful of the squalid violence and black absurdity of civil war. There is Sana, aged 13, who says: "I was a fighter for the Muslims. They used to put us at the front when the fighting started. I was so scared that I ran away to the Serbian side of the village, to come here. I am still frightened, but I feel safer."

Then there is Igor, the Serbian soldier and guard whose uncle was killed last week, and who says: "I have my old schoolfriends and my teacher in there," and then introduces his old pal Azmir, a professional footballer, from behind the wire. "I was taken here from Rizvanovici, after the fighting started," says Azmir. "There was some shooting from the Muslim side, then the police came and took the people away, to clear the village of Muslims and to do the fighting."

The situation is, says Azmir, that he can leave only if his family arrive to claim him, or if he can produce some sort of guarantee or transit papers. "But how am I supposed to do that?" The authorities claim they are organising such papers, as they have done at other camps inside Serbia. (One "concentration camp" on the Muslim list at Subotica is, in effect, a transit centre for issuing papers. Last Friday, it contained eight Turks charged with drugs trafficking.)

But in the chaos, it could take time enough to turn Trnopolje into a swelling nightmare.

"I do not know what to do, or where my mother and father are," Azmir says.

"It is not easy to think about what on earth we are doing here."

The landscape from which these people - in Omarska and Trnopolje - have been harvested is a desperate arena of war, destruction and human movement: prisoners and refugees from all sides. For 10 miles down the road from Prijedor to Banja Luka almost every Muslim house is gutted and empty.

In Banja Luka, itself, buses are arriving, bringing Serbs from hostile

Zagreb and the fighting in Sarajevo. They greet their relatives tearfully. "I have come to bring my parents here," says Drazna. "Although I will go back to Zagreb. It is very difficult for us there now, but I have my job, and if I lose it I cannot feed my family and aunts and uncles back here." Others had terrible stories of Muslim advances into their quarters of Sarajevo.

The Serbs will take houses belonging to Banja Luka Muslims who have either left voluntarily or been moved out. The pathetic convoy from Zagreb has crossed the battle lines under the auspices of Unprofor, the UN peacekeeping force, as will the Muslims in the opposite direction.

Jan Bolling, the UN official organising this move, is frank about the choices for those on both sides, between moving and the camps. "We are not interested in any ethnic cleansing whatsoever. But now we face the situation where we must choose between either that or straightforward persecution, and our job is first of all to protect people."

As ever in this war, there are extraordinary elements that complicate any simple interpretation. Women flock into Prijedor, carrying their children, telling how their menfolk were rounded up and taken to Omarska, Kereter or Trnopolje, and never seen again. Some villages are completely destroyed.

But down the road are other Muslim villages intact, peasants calmly bringing in the hay. Every house hangs a white flag - a piece of sheet or pillowcase - from the roof or from a tree: it is a guarantee against Omarska or Trnopolje.

"These are the people who accept the Serbian republic," explains Major Milovan Milutonic from Army HQ in Banja Luka. "If they do that, we just leave them alone."

There are Croatian communities around Banja Luka too, exchanging their docility to the new order for a relatively quiet life.

There are Serbian refugees on the move, too. Heavy fighting this week between the army and Croatians around Brcko - a Serbian town now reduced to virtual rubble - has shrunk part of the Serbian corridor through northern Bosnia to a network of dirt roads. And along those dirt roads last Tuesday, groups of refugees gathered with their few belongings in the dust thrown up by juggernauts, waiting for trucks and buses to take them back to their refugee camps in Serbia.

Then there is the Serbian counter-argument to the accusations of concentration camps.

Firstly, that of Milan Kovacevic, who, as president of the executive council of Prijedor, is technically responsible for Omarska and Trnopolje. He was born in Jasenovac, the Croatian Ustashe camp where 750,000 Serbs and Jews were killed between 1941 and 1945.

"We know what is a concentration camp, better than the English," he says.

"Many of us passed through them, and what you will see here is not a concentration camp. We are accused of genocide. There is no genocide."

That was before the abrupt end to the visit to Omarska. "And also please remember we are at war," he adds. "The civilians will be provided with documents and can leave. The soldiers will be investigated and tried."

The Serbs have their own list of "concentration camps" where they claim their people are also being held and killed by Croatian and Muslim authorities.

Private correspondence from the Serbian-Bosnian government to the International Red Cross refers to them as "alleged detention centres".

However, the Serbian authorities complain that the Western media have made no attempt to discover what the conditions are like in camps on the other side.

The principal camps on the Serb list are at Tarcin, near Sarajevo, various underground locations in Sarajevo, in the beseiged town of Tuzla still held by Muslims, the soccer stadium at Bihac and an underground camp at Zenica. The Serbian army in Sarajevo claims that its siege of Gorazde is held in check by the fact that the Muslims have 3,000 Serbs held hostage behind the defensive lines.

Appendix 2 – 'The Proof'

Daily Mail (London)

August 7, 1992, Friday

SECTION: Pg. 1, 2

LENGTH: 1374 words

HEADLINE: THE PROOF; BEHINH THE BARBED WIRE,THE BRUTAL TRUTH ABOUT THE SUFFERING IN BOSNIA

BODY:

THE ribs stand out so far you can almost see the bare bone straining against the emaciated flesh.

The sunken eyes stare with a mixture of bewilderment and beseeching inquiry from behind the strands of barbed wire.

They are the sort of scenes which flicker in black and white images from 50-year-old films of Nazi concentration camps.

But these pictures were taken this week in the brutal camps that Serbs have set up to hold their hated Moslem enemies in Bosnia.

The men are so thin, explain the Serbs, because of the shortage of food in a country torn by war. They cannot explain why the guards and the officials sent by their leader Radovan Karadzic look well-fed, even plump.

The men who crowd to the wire to see if the observers might be from the Red Cross or United Nations on a mission to save them, or maybe just bring them food, are disappointed.

Their visitors are journalists, from ITN, Channel 4 News and The Guardian who can only spread the news of their plight to the rest of the world.

In some ways the men with the haunted eyes, the stubbled lantern jaws and the close-cropped heads are the lucky ones. At least they are still on their feet.

Rolls of film smuggled out of the camps show how some of the inmates have been savagely beaten. One man's skeletal back is a red mass of bloody weals.

A Moslem doctor, asked if beatings have taken place, looks anxiously about him and then nods. When he is asked if there have been many beatings, his expression is the only answer necessary.

One man asked the film crews to return again in a few days to make sure that the act of speaking to them had not cost him his life.

ITN reporter Penny Marshall, Channel 4's Ian Williams and Ed Vulliamy of The Guardian were escorted to two camps in Northern Bosnia.

The first, a disused mine at Omarska, looked as if some kind of madness had suddenly come across an ordinary industrial estate.

Lines of scarecrow figures jog 30 at a time from the metal sheds that are their prison huts to the canteen where they take their single meal of the day.

A well-built, well-fed guard, cradling a machine gun, gazes down from a glass observation tower.

Inside the canteen, the prisoners - said by the Serbs to be captured enemy soldiers - scrape hungrily with their spoons at a thin and watery bean stew.

Blackened teeth tear at hunks of bread.

There is no conversation. The men gaze at the group of journalists in mute appeal. Five minutes later, the meal is over and the men - some still clutching pieces of bread which they will savour later - jog back to their quarters.

The camera crews are forbidden to look inside, despite the entreaty that Karadzic had said that the smallest corner should be open to scrutiny.

The officials in charge of the camps - local police forces which are a law unto themselves - simply shrug and marshal the next 30 prisoners for their meal.

One inmate, Sebakoudin Elezovic, told Ed Vulliamy: 'Every day is the same, like this, just doing nothing and waiting to eat. The old people and children move on, I don't know where.'

Somewhere down the road lines of wives and children queue up to be registered as refugees. At least they are still on the right side of the barbed wire.

A few miles away, a camp at Trnopolje is supposed to be where innocent men - not being transferred to military prisoner of war camps in Serbia itself – are taken.

But if anything the treatment here is far worse than anything even the most pessimistic politician had feared.

The camp, based on a former school, is a grim, ramshackle compound where the men stand stripped to the waist in the 100 degree heat. There are women and children here too.

Their village, Kozarac, has been razed to the ground. It is all part of the process of 'ethnic cleansing'.

ITN reporter Penny Marshall said many of the prisoners in the camps were too terrified to speak. 'They were very underfed and in a very bad mental and physical condition,' she said. 'It was enough to suggest that serious investigation needs to be done immediately.'

Dr Karadzic told Channel 4 last night that he would investigate the claims, although the journalists say he has no control over what is going on.

'The people responsible for this will be punished,' he claimed.

Appendix 3 – 'Iran vows to help end Genocide'

The Guardian (London)

August 7, 1992

SECTION: THE GUARDIAN FOREIGN PAGE; Pg. 6

LENGTH: 372 words

HEADLINE: IRAN VOWS TO HELP END 'GENOCIDE'

BYLINE: MICHAEL SIMMONS

BODY:

IRAN'S president, Hashemi Rafsanjani, said yesterday his country was ready to co-operate with other Islamic countries to end the "savage massacre" of Muslims in Bosnia-Herzegovina.

"Muslim countries and international organisations are responsible towards this genocide," Tehran Radio quoted him as telling the Bosnian foreign minister, Haris Silajdzic.

"The Islamic Republic of Iran is ready for all co-operation with Muslim countries and international bodies to end the savage massacre of innocent and defenceless Muslims in Bosnia-Herzegovina," he added.

Mr Rafsanjani promised Mr Silajdzic that Iran would meet Bosnia-Herzegovina's winter fuel needs, Tehran Radio said.

On Wednesday, Iran asked the Organisation of the Islamic Conference to hold an emergency meeting to study military options to defend Bosnian Muslims against Serb attacks.

The deputy foreign minister, Mahmoud Vaezi, has also urged the Nonaligned Movement to take "effective steps" to end the war. Iran has threatened to boycott the next Nonaligned summit - in Jakarta next month - if Yugoslavia keeps its place as chairman.

An Iranian fact-finding delegation will visit Bosnia and is expected to recommend that Iran send more humanitarian aid. An Iranian student killed in the fighting in Sarajevo has already been declared a martyr by the authorities in Tehran.

Mr Silajdzic, who represented Bosnian and Muslim interests at a London peace conference last week, has told the Iranians that Bosnia was not being treated very seriously.

Islamic foreign ministers have agreed, with Saudi Arabian backing, to support military intervention if sanctions against Serbia failed to work.

- The Pope has joined in the arguments about concentration camps in Serbian-held areas. An aide said yesterday that the Vatican agreed there were parallels between Nazism and human rights abuses in Bosnia.

The Archbishop of Zagreb, Franjo Kuharic, had provided firm evidence of atrocities committed against Croats and Muslims, he added. "The Pope welcomes all the initiatives taken by the United Nations and the European states to put a brake on the horrendous war," the Vatican's secretary of state, Angelo Sodano, said yesterday.

Appendix 4 – 'Butcher Moves in for the Kill'

Daily Mail (London)

July 13, 1995

SECTION: Pg. 1, 7

LENGTH: 1440 words

HEADLINE: BUTCHER MOVES IN FOR THE KILL;

(1) Genocide fear as ethnic cleansing truck rolls in (2) FAMISHED AND TERRIFIED, MOSLEM REFUGEES ARE HERDED OUT OF SREBRENICA (3) Convoy of cruelty

BODY:

RACKED by fear and hunger, they thought they had found a haven in the hell of Bosnia.

But yesterday, in the sinister shape of General Ratko Mladic, the shadow of death fell on 40,000 Moslem refugees in Srebrenica.

With chilling echoes of the Nazi Holocaust, the brutal Serb commander - named as a war criminal - went in to claim the spoils of victory: Wretched hordes of helpless men, women and children ripe for ethnic cleansing.

As his forces tightened their iron grip on the captured United Nations 'safe haven' - and the West bickered over what to do next - the refugees were packed aboard trucks and buses for what could be a journey to genocide. The terrifying plan by the Butcher of Bosnia was to transport men over 16 to a football stadium in the Serb-held town of Bratunac. There, they would be screened to identify those Mladic described as 'possible war criminals'. Few observers doubted that many 'possible war criminals' would be found. And there were no illusions about the fate that awaited them.

Stephan Oberreit of the medical charity Medecins Sans Frontieres, who saw the forced exodus, said: 'There was a horrible scene of screaming. Women and children were put aside to be loaded on to buses while young men were put in other places. Obviously this loading of buses was terrifying. People were screaming and panicking.

'Those people were in a terrible state of fright and despair - very tired, lacking everything, no shelter. Sanitation conditions were terrible.' Bosnian Serb television showed about 20,000 refugees, mostly frightened and confused women, children and the elderly, waiting to board the buses and trucks in Potocari, north of Srebrenica.

Mladic was seen approaching a boy. He patted him on the head and asked his name, then told the refugees: 'You don't have to be afraid of anything. No one will harm you. In this first round we will evacuate women, children and elderly and all those who want to leave this combat area without forcing them.

Srebrenica is free now, but there are still small groups trying to put up resistance.'

But Bosnian Serb political leader Radovan Karadzic summed up the true attitude to the captured 'safe haven' - and those in it - when he declared yesterday: 'Srebrenica is our country. It was simply a terrorist stronghold and we couldn't tolerate it any longer.'

The herding of the refugees was a sickening reminder of scenes three years ago, when Moslems from towns and villages conquered by Serbs were held in squalid camps where thousands were tortured. Thousands more women were reported raped as the Serbs advanced. Mladic arrived with his convoy yesterday to find thousands of terrified refugees pressed inside a disused battery factory and thousands more gathered outside. About 400 Dutch UN peacekeepers - who had been charged with protecting Srebrenica but were helpless in the face of the invaders - had enough food to feed the Moslems for one day and supplemented the meagre supplies with their own rations. As Mladic's round-up began, UN official Alexander Ivanko said in Sarajevo: 'We are told he is not taking No for an answer.' Bosnian

Serb officials promised 1,500 blankets, 1,200 mattresses and two tons of canned fish to the famished refugees. Few believed the pledge.

The first 1,000 were shipped out in mid-afternoon. 'This is deplorable,' said another UN official in the neighbouring 'safe haven' of Tuzla to the north-west. 'We are talking about people badly in need of medicine and food who have had nothing to eat for 24 hours and more.'

By last night, up to 3,000 civilians - mostly women, children and the elderly - had been transported from Srebrenica in two lines of buses and trucks, according to the official.

They were apparently bound for government-held Kladanj, about 30 miles west of Srebrenica, with some peacekeepers accompanying them 'to ensure that the refugees don't suffer any more', said Ivanko. 'We have been able to negotiate to have at least one Dutch UN soldier on every truck to try to monitor for any human rights abuses,' he added.

The convoys were due to stop at the front line separating Serb and government-held territory, from where the exhausted refugees would have to walk the final ten miles.

But it was the fate of the men over 16, destined to be 'screened' as war criminals that gave rise to the most apprehension. Mladic - himself named by the UN as involved in war crimes - was clearly searching in particular for Moslem guerilla chieftain Nasir Oric, who has fought a campaign that has killed scores of Serbs in east Bosnia over the last three years. Aid workers said Oric's fighters had disappeared, probably into the hills overlooking Srebrenica.

Mr Oberreit said it was vital that the Serbs were prevented from dividing the refugees into groups of men, women and children without international supervision.

He added: 'All the people are very tired and very shocked. People are just sitting staring. There is not enough water.'

As the Serbs finalised their takeover of Srebrenica, the Dutch peacekeepers - based in the Potocari battery factory - endured further humiliation. Several were taken hostage, then the invaders drove their tanks up to the door of their headquarters to ram home who was boss.

Last night, as the UN Security Council demanded a Serb withdrawal, the response in the West looked unlikely to deliver swift help to the victims of Srebrenica. And the terrifying spectre of ethnic cleansing was once more stalking Bosnia.

Appendix 5 – 'Exodus of Bosnia's damned'

Daily Mail (London)

July 15, 1995

SECTION: Pg. 20, 21

LENGTH: 614 words

HEADLINE: Exodus of Bosnia's damned; As tide of human misery swells, one girl is driven to suicide by her suffering

BODY:

SHE was about 20. Simply clad in a red cardigan and summer dress.

No one knew her name. But last night, she had become an horrific symbol of the despair of the Bosnian Moslem refugees.

As 20,000 hungry, helpless souls - women, children and frail old men – were herded like cattle from their homes in Srebrenica in the ruthless wave of Serb ethnic cleansing, she simply could not cope with the unbelievable anguish of it all.

What pushed her to her terrible fate may never be known. Many suspected she was one of scores of women said to have been raped by the Serbs. Around her, girls the same age raised their faces towards where Heaven was supposed to be, and wailed uncontrollably for kidnapped menfolk they will probably never see again.

Amidst all this, the girl in the red cardigan got up and walked away from Tuzla air base carrying a blanket. There was no one to stop her, no one to care.

Through the floods of bitter tears washing over everybody else, no one even saw her final, pitiful trek.

In woods at the edge of the airfield, she took the blanket - just about the only comfort aid workers had been able to give her - cut off a strip, and tied it to a tree. Then, driven to God only knows what depths of despair, the girl in the red cardigan hanged herself.

For hours yesterday, there was no one to cut her down, to show her kindness even in death. United Nations officials said they were aware of the tragedy.

But, as one put it: 'Let's take care of the living.'

Yet for the living, there was little succour. Dressed in rags, ravaged by hunger and thirst, haunted by the spectre of genocide, thousands trekked wearily into Tuzla and Potocari.

In scenes terrifyingly reminiscent of humanity's darkest hour - the Nazi Holocaust - they came seeking sanctuary from evil, pathetic beyond description.

In the baking heat, mothers clutched whimpering babies. Other women pushed the elderly in wheelbarrows. Hollow faces were pale with shock and fatigue, eyes blank with disbelief.

And last night, as the world looked on in impotent fury at the bloody rampage of the Serb legions, it could yet be that the fate of the girl in the red cardigan makes her one of the lucky ones.

Appendix 6 – 'Lonely death in a crowded cornfield'

The Guardian (London)
July 15, 1995

SECTION: THE GUARDIAN FOREIGN PAGE; Pg. 12

LENGTH: 2267 words

HEADLINE: LONELY DEATH IN A CROWDED CORNFIELD;
Women and girls appear to have been pulled off buses by rebel soldiers as they crossed frontline checkpoints. Aid workers said a pattern of systematic rape was emerging from accounts

BYLINE: Julian Borger

BODY:

IN A crowd of more than 10,000 refugees sprawled across Tuzla's cornfields, a young woman hanged herself yesterday.

No one knew her name. No one wept for her when her body was cut down from a tree, and only a single, bored policeman kept vigil over the corpse as it lay abandoned by the gate of the heaving, sweating camp.

She died in bare feet which protruded, white and muddy, from a thin blue blanket someone had draped over her. She had taken a black cloth belt from her dress and plaited it with a brown shawl into a makeshift noose.

Its lethal loop was still fastened around her neck, and its brown-black tail snaked across her shroud.

She had been one of the scatterlings of Europe, torn away more than once from friends, relatives and familiar places. First, when the Serbs went on a killing spree in 1992.

Now it had happened a second time, in Srebrenica, a place the United Nations had said was safe.

Most of the men had been imprisoned, girls dragged off refugee buses to be raped, and children lost in the panic.

The crowd surged back and forth past the forgotten corpse. In its midst, a young woman was weeping and kneading her hands as she walked, an older one following a few paces behind.

"I told you to keep an eye on the children, I told you not to let them out of your sight," the older one said.

The younger woman nearly buckled in misery. "I know you did, but I can't do everything," she cried.

A few hundred tents had been set up overnight, and the UN High Commissioner for Refugees (UNHCR) was sending a few thousand more, but most people in the camp had spent the night outdoors. They propped up improvised shelters by stretching blankets on leafy branches torn from trees. A few red fire trucks appeared and the crowd rushed to taps on either side to fill their water containers.

But apart from the cisterns and police, there was little sign of Bosnian government help.

UN officials - much criticised for their apparent lack of preparedness for the flood of refugees - said the Bosnian government had not only failed to contribute to the relief effort, but had even hindered it.

They said that earlier in the week the UNHCR had earmarked a number of schools and warehouses to be used as temporary shelter if Srebrenica fell, but they had been refused permission to use them by the regional government acting on orders from Sarajevo.

Crowds of women and teenagers brought on trucks from Tuzla by Bosnian government officials blockaded UN bases in and around the town for much of this week, UN sources said.

"I think they were trying to make it impossible for the refugees to be brought from Srebrenica because that would mean the end of the enclave," a senior UN military officer in Tuzla said.

"When it was clear people were going to be forced out, the government saw a symbolic value in heaping them all on the UN's lap.

"They could all have been easily dispersed to different shelters. This has created a problem," he said.

No government official was available for comment yesterday, but it appeared the local authorities had relented in the face of the enormity of the problem.

After negotiations between Bosnian officials, the UN and the UNHCR, by late afternoon six busloads of refugees could be seen moving from the UN camp at Tuzla's airfield towards the town.

But for those who remained, conditions were still desperate. Sefika Becirovic had spent the night with her two daughters on the edge of a maize field. Since being bussed out of Srebrenica early on Thursday morning, they had had nothing to eat but a tin of beans handed out yesterday at dawn.

"Better to finish us off now than leave us like this," Mrs Becirovic said.

Her husband Abdullah was 60 and blind and deaf, but the Serbs had taken him anyway.

"I shouted at them to stop, but they told me to shut up or they would find some use for me as well. I said nothing and they took him," she said.

Someone had told her he had been seen on one of the later buses.

She had positioned herself directly opposite the airfield's main gate, in the hope that would give her the best chance of seeing him.

Women and girls appear to have been pulled off buses by rebel soldiers as they crossed frontline checkpoints. Aid workers who talked to refugees said a pattern of systematic rape was emerging.

She and her daughters, Sabaheta, aged 23, and Sadeta, aged 20, were put on a bus with other women and children to the frontline.

They said Serb soldiers boarded the bus at a checkpoint, took their pick of women and dragged them off.

Sabaheta was saved by her luggage: "They pulled me by my wrist but my bag wedged between the seats and I was blocked. So they took two other women, a girl of about 19 and a woman with a child who was crying for help."

That pattern was confirmed by many other eyewitness accounts.

Women and girls appear to have been pulled off buses by rebel soldiers as they crossed frontline checkpoints. Aid workers who talked to refugees said a pattern of systematic rape was emerging.

The Red Cross yesterday began trying to trace the missing people.

By yesterday morning the flow of refugees across the frontline had stopped, leaving thousands of residents of Srebrenica unaccounted for. In the village of Ravne, 30 miles south of Tuzla, aid workers and Bosnian army soldiers waited in vain at the mouth of a narrow ravine for fresh waves of refugees to cross.

Alvin Gonzaga, a UNHCR worker manning a Land Rover at the scene said:

"Twelve thousand have crossed so far and there were thought to be between 30,000 and 40,000 people in Srebrenica before, so that's a lot of people missing."

Thousands of men and boys from Srebrenica have been held in the Serb-held town of Bratunac, together with 60 Dutch UN peacekeepers. The 400 UN soldiers still in Srebrenica have refused to leave without the refugees.

The last report sent from the enclave by UN military observers late on Thursday night said the rebels had taken the UN outpost's armoured vehicles and equipment.

It said that Bosnian Serb soldiers were systematically looting the town.

The report, clearly written under strain, departed from the usual clipped military vocabularly to describe conditions at the outpost. "The place really looks like a pigsty. The shit is even on the walls. The smell is unbearable and really an inhuman situation to live in for more days," the report said.

"Tears were in our eyes when seeing the desperate displaced persons with no secure future looking at us and seeking help we cannot give them. We really lost this enclave and our heads.

"We feel very sad that we were not able to do more," it said.

Srebrenica's new Serb rulers were crowing over their victory.

Bosnian Serb radio announced: "Normality has been restored to 'Free Srebrenica'," and broadcast a song which the presenter said was being sung throughout the enclave. It was a peasants' song, a wailing melody without discernible words chanted in men's voices.

A few minutes later, another song was played.

Sounding like a football chant, its words were: "Die you scum, the Serbs are the champions. Come out on to your balconies and hail the white Serb race."

Appendix 7 – 'For Whom does the Bell Toll Now?'

The Guardian (London)

July 15, 1995

SECTION: THE GUARDIAN FEATURES PAGE; Pg. 23

LENGTH: 3067 words

HEADLINE: FOR WHOM DOES THE BELL TOLL NOW?

The left buried its differences to fight fascism directly in the Spanish civil war. Now, says ED VULLIAMY, it has a range of reactions to Bosnia and is mostly agreed that we should keep out.

BYLINE: Ed Vulliamy

BODY:

SIXTY years ago, Generalissimo Franco, backed by the Axis powers, assaulted the Spanish Republic. The response on the left in Europe and America was famously unequivocal: it buried the nit-picking differences and rallied to the cause, the defeat of fascism. Thousands put their lives where their mouths were, and fought.

It took time for the British left to absorb what was going on. The Labour Party was wary, opposed to intervening in another country's business. Although the International Brigades answered the call, the Republic fought alone, and perished.

In three years, there was a replay of the interventionist debate, over Czechoslovakia, and the word appeasement replaced non-intervention in the diplomatic vocabulary, courtesy of a Conservative government, and a promise secured in Munich.

This week, the Serbian nationalist juggernaut rolled again, into the worst ethnic cleansing since the terrifying summer of 1992. The Government's response has been, predictably, laissez-bloodbath. The more curious reaction has been on the left, where there have been remarkable displays of political acrobatics throughout the Bosnian war.

Bosnia is deemed too complicated to understand, its complications hidden from comprehension by Balkan history. Any attempt to simplify the war into a tragedy of aggression, resistance and betrayal is muddied by pedantry and disinformation, usually from UN sources (as in "the Muslims bombed their own marketplace . . .") On the British left, the confusion falls on willing ears, for in this - it is said - there is nothing so simple as Spain in the thirties.

The savagery provokes cacaphonous views: some even speak as political ambassadors for ethnic violence. "The result," says Callum Mcdonald, Labour MP for the Western Isles, "is that the left has miserably failed Bosnia."

In Sarajevo, Tuzla and what is left of rural Bosnia, the victims understandably define the concentration camps, the forced movement of populations, the destruction of communities - and what is happening in Srebrenica - as fascism. "If a systematic programme to destroy a people and their history isn't fascism," said Brigadier Selmo Cikotic, former commander in central Bosnia, now military attache in Washington, "then I don't know what is."

That view is shared by titans of British radicalism, like Michael Foot, who brands Bosnia "the great anti-fascist war of your generation." The young Callum McDonald sees Bosnia as "Spain, Abyssinia and Czechoslovakia rolled into one. It is as clear to me how the left should react to Bosnia, as it was to Hitlerism in the thirties." These are not the thirties - when those who travelled hopefully felt able to stake a claim in the future - but years of ambition rather than risk, of hesitant complexity rather than simple goals. The very words left and right are melting into each other.

If we thought that the defeat of the Third Reich meant that the bullies of history need not triumph in Europe, we were wrong. But one dividing line persists: between those who believe in defying the evils, and those who shrug or smudge the horrors with words.

Bosnia has splintered rather than united the left - divided radicals and conservatives from their usual fellow-travellers - and created some curious trans-ideological alliances. In the "do-something-this -is-intolerable" camp, Michael Foot alongside Margaret Thatcher. On the "do-nothing-they're-all-as-bad-as-each -other" side, the Revolutionary Communist Party right alongside Douglas Hurd and Malcolm Rifkind. There is nothing new in this: after Stalin and Hitler signed a pact over Poland, fascism was opposed by communists and Gaullists in France, by both red partisans and Christians in Italy. Now comes the most extraordinary alliance: Tony Benn and a chunk of the British left alongside Sir Alfred Sherman, former speechwriter to Mrs Thatcher, confidant to Jean-Marie Le Pen and until recently advisor to the Bosnian Serb tin god, Radovan Karadzic. On a platform with Benn recently, Sherman declared himself proud to have served Karadzic; Benn lambasted the "Foot-Thatcher axis".

The Labour Party has splintered over Bosnia, "although most," says McDonald, "are apathetic. I despair that the left thinks in terms of what is trendy. It was trendy to campaign for the abolition of apartheid in South Africa, but not to oppose the creation of apartheid in Europe."

In Parliament, it was left to Paddy Ashdown's Liberals to speak for Bosnia's frontiers, her victims, and to urge action in their defence, while Labour imitated the Government in crisis management through empty bluff. The partnership of Jack Cunningham (shadow Foreign) and David Clarke (shadow Defence) was anti -interventionist, treating it as civil war between barbarians.

The shadow defence team is the most sceptical, with John Reid arguing that Serbs had legitimate grievances, wary of what he regarded as Islamic influence in Bosnia. (A place where attendance at mosque was three per cent, where "Muslims" drink brandy with their bacon.) When Robin Cook became shadow Foreign, Labour's voice changed. Cook argued that Bosnia is riven between warring principles, and set down codes to replace the fixation with maps and partition. Among MPs, there are supporters of the Sarajevo government, most wanting tougher intervention on Bosnia's behalf: including Macdonald, Ken Livingstone, Chris Mullin and Peter Mandelson. Then there are neutrals: Tony Benn, Denis Skinner, Diane Abbot, Bob Waring, Alice Mahon

These last are the Committee for Peace in Balkans, formed last month to oppose further commitment of troops. It brought together leading members of Labour's left and CND - and Sir Alf Sherman. Tony Benn says it is "a peace movement". It won't hear criticism of Serbian pogroms in Bosnia, and refuses to call them such.

Sections of the British left stubbornly believe "nothing can be done" about the slaughter: they range from genteel Fabian salons to the muscular hard left, from the revolutionary fringes to the front benches. They have blended little-Englandism, anti-imperialism, appeasement, an idea that whoever governs in Belgrade and Moscow must by tradition be socialist, and a basic belief that whatever the Americans think must be wrong - and America is deemed to support Bosnia.

Underlying this is fond nostalgia for the second world war - with animosity towards Croatia, coupled with instinctive affection for our war-time ally, Belgrade. The Serbian Nazi puppet regime and Chetnik support for Hitler are overlooked.

Benn is angry that in compiling its guest lists for VE Day, "the British government invited the Croatians, who fought on the Nazi side, and they didn't invite Serbia, which was our ally." There is keen hostility towards modern Germany. Dennis Skinner brings a conversation about Bosnia back to his theme of "the German high command" scheming within the EU and the Balkans to establishm"the new German empire".

Tony Benn believes "the break-up of Yugoslavia was a deliberate act of German policy to re-assert control in the Balkans . . . starting with the unilateral recognition of Croatia." The Bosnian cause is regarded as inseparable from that of Croatia, although the Muslim-Croat federation was prefaced by 16 months of war in which Zagreb helped the Bosnian Croats try to annexe their slice of Bosnia, supplying heavy weaponry for the siege of Mostar's Muslim enclave.

There is inevitable identification with Tito's Yugoslavia, for some reason embodied by present-day Serbia. "I would like to see," says Skinner, "a return to old Yugoslavia." So would most Bosnians on the government side - Serb, Croat and Muslim. They regard the ethnically pluralist country for which they fight as heir to Tito's republic. "It was not Bosnia that seceded from the idea of Yugoslavia," says Brigadier Cikotic, " Serbia did that."

But the crucial left premise is a refusal among the neutrals to acknowledge any difference of scale between atrocities committed by the combatants. Exactly reflecting the Government's treatment of aggressor and victim as equals, this is the doctrine of "moral equivalence", rejected by the UN Commission on War Crimes under Dr Cherif Boussani, not alone in blaming nationalist Serbs for most war crimes.

But for the neutrals, the ethnic cleansing across Bosnia, the camps, the bombardment of Sarajevo are compared with "Muslim atrocities". Such atrocities have occured - a few isolated, wild, excursions out of Gorazde and Srebrenica.

"Are you suggesting that there haven't been atrocities on both sides?" barks Skinner. "It's happening on all sides, and there is ethnic cleansing right here, of miners in the pits, so don't tell me about ethnic cleansing."

The core principle of the left neutrals is also that of Serbian dogma: that neither Bosnia nor - more importantly - Bosnians exist. "It's a civil war, however you look at it," says Benn. Now the argument comes straight from Belgrade, where it is held that the Bosnians are in fact "Serbs of Muslim faith". "It wasn't ethnic cleansing," says Benn, "A lot of the Muslims are Serbs who became Muslims because the Turks were there." An identical argument was used by the Croats and their blood brothers when they began to carve out their corner of Bosnia in 1992. "There is no such thing as a Bosnian Muslim," said the hardline Bosnian-Croat leader Mate Boban, "they are Croats of Muslim faith."

Not all the new group are willing to discuss their views. Diane Abbot, another sponsor, flatly refused to explain her affiliation. "It baffles and depresses me", says Callum Macdonald. "This is so obviously our cause, the fight against fascism on our doorstep. What these people are doing is like supporting the Nazis in France because Napoleon was French. It is a complete failure to read the lessons of the past into the present'.

Out on the revolutionary left, there is teeming debate: this time round, the line is anti-interventionist, in some sects even pro-Serbian, in others staunchly pro-Bosnian. The group most adept at winning Channel Four airspace is the Revolutionary Communist Party, whose Balkan specialist Joan Phillips says that "our criticism of the West is that it has intervened too much," and that "this is a civil war. . . I do not accept for a minute that the Serbs should be singled out as responsible."This company is hotly challenged by the Workers Revolutionary Party, which urges resistance to Karadzic to avert "the first victory for fascism in Europe since the Third Reich." The group's paper is one of the few crannies of British coverage recording those Serbs who remain loyal to, and fight for, what is called the Muslim side. The latest 'Workers Press' carries an enthusiastic review of a new book called Genocide In Bosnia, acknowledging that the author is "not a socialist. Indeed, he is a professor of national security studies at the US Marine school of advanced warfighting!"

"In some ways," concludes Michael Foot, "the ethnic cleansing in Bosnia is worse than Franco in Spain. Franco destroyed socialists and liberals. But this is a doctrine with a racial basis . . . So the non-interventionists are even more culpable than they were in the thirties. If there had not been those non -interventionists on the left then I have no doubt that the Spanish republic would have survived".

My friend Bojan Zec (mixed Serbian, Jewish and Muslim - a real Bosnian) said this in Sarajevo, two years ago: "For us, this is a war against fascism. For us, Sarajevo is the Madrid of our time, but not for you. Perhaps the failure to help us generated your attitude. Your anti-fascist war came and went, and you did nothing - and therefore you have to call it anything but an anti-fascist war, and to leave us alone to face the fascism of our day."

"Did you pick up a gun and fight?" says Denis Skinner down the telephone.

Fair challenge. "You could have done, but you didn't, did you? No. You wrote an article for the newspaper instead."